THE HERMITAGE

Alfa Colour Art Publishers
2008

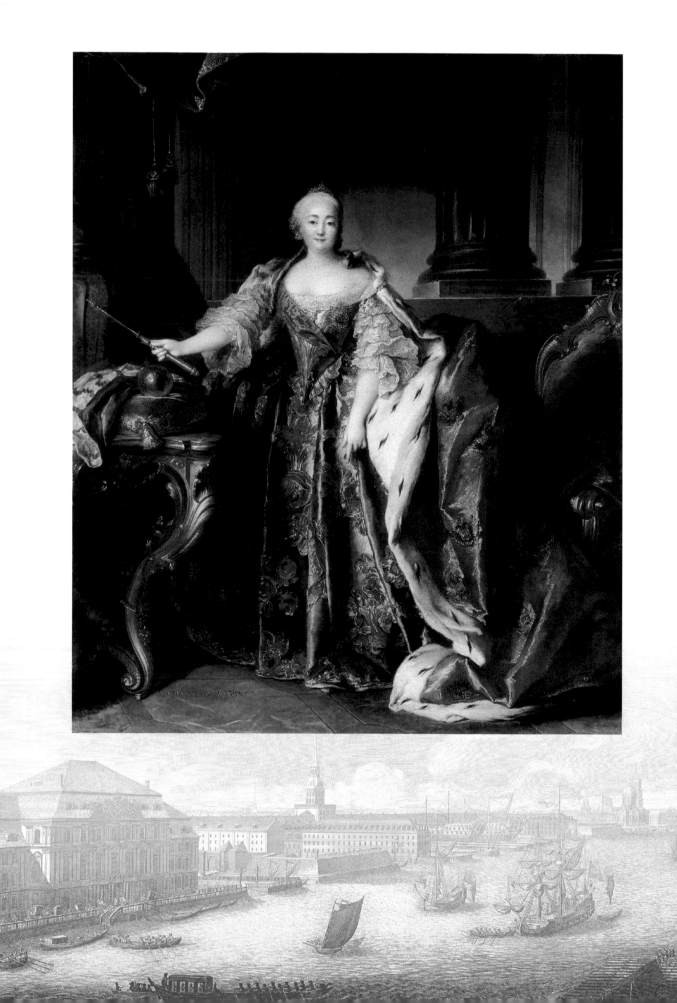

The State Hermitage is the largest museum of Russia, the collection of which numbers about three millions exhibits, including works of painting, sculpture, graphic and applied art, archaeological finds, coins and medals.

The Hermitage collection has been formed in the course of three centuries. Some of the masterpieces preserved in the museum have been acquired in the early eighteenth century, in the reign of Peter the Great. In the second half of the same century art collecting made an amazing progress in Russia. Thus, Catherine the Great, in addition to individual works and small groups of canvases, purchased several large collections that made up the core of the picture gallery of the present-day museum. The earliest in this series of large-scale acquisitions was the former collection of the Berlin merchant Johann Ernst Gotzkowsky including 225 paintings by Western European masters that was received as a compensation of his debt to the Russian court in 1764. This year is taken to be the date of the foundation of the Hermitage.

During the nineteenth and twentieth centuries the collection continued to grow thanks to numerous purchases, archaeological finds, and gifts as well as thanks to the works transferred from other Russian museums. The Hermitage collections continue to grow to this day.

Today the exhibitions of the Hermitage occupy several buildings. The earliest of them is the Winter Palace that was the main residence of the Russian Emperors for a century and a half. Located on the shore of the Neva, in the very heart of St Petersburg, the palace was erected in 1754–62 by Francesco Bartolomeo Rastrelli (1700–1771) by orders of Empress Elizabeth, daughter of Peter the Great. In the first half of the eighteenth century several imperial winter residences had replaced one another and the new Winter Palace occupied the site of the former royal building, constructed in 1732–35 by Francesco Bartolomeo Rastrelli and his father, Bartolomeo Carlo Rastrelli (1675–1744) for Empress Anna Ioannovna.

Louis Tocquet (1696–1772)
Portrait of Empress Elizabeth Petrovna. 1758

Lucas Conrad Pfandzelt (1716–1788)
Portrait of the Architect
Franceso Bartolomeo Rastrelli. 1750s–1760s

View of the Neva in the Middle
of the Eighteenth Century
From a drawing of Mikhail Makhayev.
Left, the old Winter Palace
of Empress Anna Ioannovna

The Winter Palace.
Architect: Francesco Bartolomeo Rastrelli. 1754–62

The Northern Pavilion of the Small Hermitage.
Architect: Jean-Baptiste Vallin de La Mothe. 1767–69

Vigilius Ericksen (1722–1782). *Portrait*
of Catherine the Great in Front of a Mirror. **1762–64**

An Italian by birth, Rastrelli the Junior came to the banks of the Neva at the age of sixteen with his father. His formation as an artist took place primarily at the construction of St Petersburg and its environs. The Winter Palace is one of the best achievements of Elizabeth's court architect, the most brilliant master of the Russian Baroque. This grand edifice, symbolizing the majesty of the Russian Empire, dominated by its dimensions and luxury the central part of the capital that had just celebrated its fiftieth anniversary.

Even today the Baroque grandeur of the Winter Palace singles it out among more austere classical buildings. The fronts of the palace, divided into two tiers, are decorated with numerous snow-white columns clearly standing out against the green walls, the reliefs of which are enriched with luxurious and varied moulded window surrounds. Numerous statues and vases crown the building making its silhouette more elaborate.

Elizabeth died in 1762, before the completion of her new Winter Palace. In the reign of Catherine the Great the Elizabethan Baroque, however, was ousted by Classicism. Rastrelli was retired, although he had not yet completed the inner décor of the palace. Within the same, eighteenth century, the interiors were gradually redesigned in keeping with the new tastes by Jean-Baptiste Vallin de La Mothe (1729–1800), Antonio Rinaldi (1709?–1794), Yury Velten (1730–1801), Giacomo Quarenghi (1744–1817) and Ivan Starov (1745–1808). Eight crowned owners replaced one another in the Winter Palace in the course of its existence as a royal residence. The interiors of this structure illustrate the history of Russian and St Petersburg

architecture from the middle of the eighteenth to the early twentieth century. Tastes and style changed and the décor of the halls and rooms changed with them. Active in the palace in the nineteenth century were such outstanding architects as Carlo Rossi (1775–1849), Auguste de Montferrand (1786–1858), Andrei Stackenschneider (1802–1865) and Harald Bosse (1812–1894).

In 1837, during the reign of Nicholas I, the palace suffered a great damage from fire. The fire erased all the inner décor of the building. The imperial residence was restored within an amazingly brief period – in fifteen months. The work was supervised by the architects Vasily Stasov (1769–1848) and Alexander Briullov (1798–1877). Stasov's task was to re-create the destroyed interiors "to their former state", whereas Briullov was to design the burnt interiors anew, in accordance with new aesthetic tastes.

The palace was the residence of the Russian Emperors until the revolution of 1917. The museum collections were arranged in it in the 1920s and 1930s.

In 1764–75, by orders of Catherine the Great, the so-called Small Hermitage was put up next to the Winter Palace, to the east of it. The building work was carried out to projects by Vallin de La Mothe and Velten. This building, the smallest in the Hermitage complex, consists of two pavilions, with a hanging garden located at the level of the first floor between two galleries. The austere and slender Northern Pavilion, erected to a design by Vallin de La Mothe, is executed according to the style of Classicism. The façade of the three-storey building, overlooking the Neva, is divided into two tiers to match the articulation of the Winter Palace. The more heavy lower tier supports a slender six-column portico. The pilasters and statues on either side of the colonnade create a soft transition from the surface of the wall to the projecting columns.

5

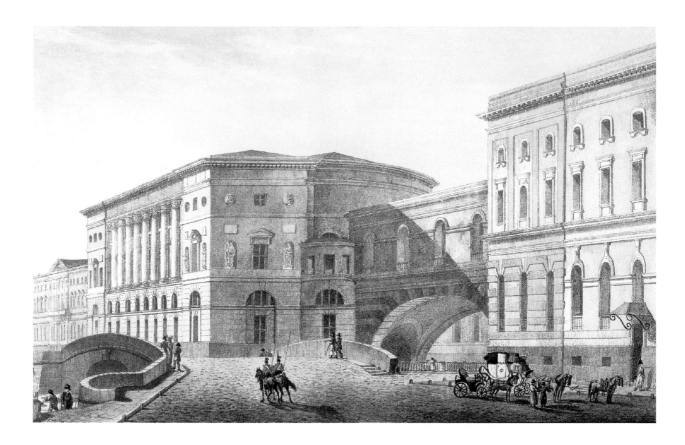

The French word *hermitage* means "a hermit's abode" or "a lonely place". The earliest pavilion bearing such name in imitation of the French fashion was built in Peter's time at Peterhof and then, in the reign of Elizabeth, such structure appeared at Tsarskoye Selo. There also existed not only separate "Hermitage" buildings, but also similar interiors in some larger residences. An indispensable element of the "Hermitage" was a table with a lifting mechanism. It enabled to spend a dinner or supper "in a seclusion", without servants. All necessary things were lifted from the ground floor by means of hand-operated mechanisms. One room on the first floor of the Northern Pavilion in the Small Hermitage also had such a device. Catherine the Great used to arrange here her "small hermitages" – parties where only the Empress's closest associates were present. Catherine compiled the rules of conduct herself. Her guests were to appear in Russian clothing, it was allowed to speak only Russian and the rules demanded "to leave all ranks and titles" at the entrance.

In the 1850s, Andrei Stackenschneider replaced eighteenth-century interiors in the Northern Pavilion with the new Pavilion Hall. On the southern side the huge windows of this hall overlook the Hanging Garden resting on the vaults of the ground floor. There were a manége and stables under its terrace in the nineteenth century. Created in the open air, the garden is protected from the wind by the Northern and Southern Pavilions and two galleries.

These galleries were intended for the hanging of paintings of the imperial collection as early as the eighteenth century and their number rapidly augmented in the reign of Catherine the Great. After the purchase of Gotzkowsky's collection were bought the famous collections of Count Heinrich von Brühl (1769, Drezden), Pierre Crozat (1772, Paris), Lord Robert Walpole (1779, Haughton Hall, England), Count de Boudouin (1781, Paris) and a number of other private collections. Acquiring art works for her collections, Catherine the Great used advice and help of the most educated people of her age both in Russia and abroad.

The growth of the collections made the construction of new premises necessary. In 1771–87 a building was erected at the Neva embankment, alongside the Winter Palace and the Small Hermitage, that came to be known as the Old Hermitage in the nineteenth century.

Besides works of painting, it housed the Empress's private library. The new building, created to a project by Yury Velten, one of major representatives of Early Classicism, did not break the harmonious duet of the buildings that had already existed on the embankment. The stretched and concise façade of the Old Hermitage highlights the plastic exuberance of the Winter Palace and the elegance of the Small Hermitage.

A passionate infatuation with theatrical performances in the eighteenth century demanded the construction of a special building attached to the royal residence. In 1783, still before the construction of the Old Hermitage had ended, Giacomo Quarenghi began to erect the Hermitage Theatre next to it, behind the Winter Canal.

View of the Hermitage Theatre and the Arch over the Winter Canal
Tinted lithograph by Carl Kollmann (1786–1846). 1820s

The Old Hermitage. Architect: Yury Velten. 1771–87

**The auditorium of the Hermitage Theatre
Architect: Giacomo Quarenghi. 1783–86**

Creating the new building the architect used the walls of the former Winter Palace of Peter the Great, put up on this site in 1716–23 to a design by the architect Georg Johann Mattarnovi (?–1719). The surviving section of the former royal residence, uncovered in the twentieth century from later accretions, is now a part of the museum display.

The Hermitage Theatre is one of the best works created by Giacomo Quarenghi, an architect of the austere Classical style. The edifice is distinguished by simplicity, clarity and commensurate proportions characteristic of this master's manner. The main accent of the front design on the embankment side is the Corinthian colonnade set back into the mass of the wall. The rounded volumes of the western front correspond to the shape of the auditorium echoing the outlines of the hump-backed Hermitage Bridge and the arch spanning the Winter Canal. Over the arch, erected by Velten in the same 1780s, is located the gallery that serves as a passageway from the Old Hermitage to the auditorium.

The auditorium was designed as an amphitheatre with six rows of benches. "I wished to give an ancient appearance to the theatre," wrote Quarenghi in the first album of his engraved drawings published in 1787. Despite numerous minor structures, the auditorium of the Hermitage Theatre has retained the overall design of its creator. The walls and columns are faced with varicoloured marble of warm shades. The Corinthian capitals of the columns bear theatrical masks. In the niches are statues of Apollo and the nine Muses. Mounted in the walls over them are medallions with profile depictions of composers and playwrights. In front of the stage are small stalls and two small boxes. One of the boxes was allotted to Quarenghi for use throughout his life. Performances, regularly staged in the theatre, were a favourite pastime of the imperial court. In the nineteenth century new-year masked balls

were arranged here. Many outstanding Russian actors of the eighteenth and nineteenth centuries, including Yelizaveta Sandunova, Fiodor Chaliapin and other, performed on the stage of the Hermitage Theatre. Nowadays ballet and opera performances as well as concerts of chamber and symphonic music are regularly held here, too.

The construction of the Hermitage Theatre completed the formation of the palace complex with its façade overlooking the cmbankment. The Neva side affords a magnificent view of the four Hermitage buildings. Although erected in different periods, they formed a brilliant architectural quartet. The luxurious Baroque of the Winter Palace perfectly blends, thanks to the similar height and basic horizontal articulations, the three buildings dating from different periods of Classicism – the Small Hermitage, the Old Hermitage and the Hermitage Theatre.

As early as the eighteenth century all the Hermitage buildings were interconnected and linked with the Winter Palace by passageways. When a disastrous fire raged in the Winter Palace in 1837, the passageways from the palace to the Small Hermitage were dismantled and the doorways were bricked up. The thus formed blind wall and all the rooms of the palace facing the museum were incessantly poured with water by firemen. As a result of these measures the fire did not spread beyond the limits of the Winter Palace.

The reign of Nicholas I was marked in the history of the museum not only by this devastating fire in the Winter Palace, but by the construction of the New Hermitage as well.

Buildings of the Hermitage. View from the Neva side

The New Hermitage is not seen from the Neva. The main, southern front of this imposing edifice faces Millionnaya Street; the eastern front overlooks the Winter Canal and the western one affords a view of a narrow lane separating it from the Small Hermitage. A picturesque view of this majestic building opens up from Millionnaya Street, from the spot where it crosses the Winter Canal.

The New Hermitage was designed in 1839–42 by the eminent German architect Leo von Klenze (1784–1864), the designer of the famous Pinakothek in Munich. The construction work lasted from 1842 to 1851 under the supervision of the Russian architects Vasily Stasov and Nikolai Yefimov (1799–1851). The New Hermitage became the earliest building in Russia put up specially for a public museum of art. The collection of Catherine the Great was the Empress's private, inaccessible possession and the buildings housing it were an integral part of the imperial residence. The Small and Old Hermitage buildings served in the eighteenth century both for the accommodation of works of art and for court pastimes – suppers, receptions and games. In the nineteenth century palatial collections were replaced in many European countries by public museums intended to make works of art accessible to everybody. The construction of the New Hermitage reflects this process in Russia. The outward and inner design of this grand-scale edifice corresponds to its designation. The powerful smooth walls of the structure, broken by large windows, are decorated with statues of famous artists, architects and sculptors of all times and peoples. While Catherine's Hermitage had a purely decorative arrangement of her paintings, in the new museum the objects were arranged with regard to ages, schools and masters. According to the concept of the architect, the arrangement of statues on the fronts was to correspond to the arrangement of

Fire in the Winter Palace in 1837
View from the Neva. **Drawing by an unknown artist. 1837**

Franz von Krüger. *Portrait of Nicholas I.* **1852**

View of the New Hermitage from Millionnaya Street
Watercolour by Luigi Premazzi (1814–1891). 1861

the collections within the museum. For example, the statues of the ancient Greek sculptors Pheidias and Skopas corresponded with the rooms of ancient art, while the figures of Raphael, Rubens and Van Dyck referred to the exhibition of painting. The famous portico with the statues of Atlantes carved in grey granite under the supervision of the sculptor Alexander Terebenev (1815–1859), which marked the main entrance to the imperial museum in the nineteenth century, became the emblem not only of this building but of the entire Hermitage complex, too. After the completion of the construction work, precious exhibits were transferred to the New Hermitage from the Small and Old Hermitage buildings. The ceremony of the inauguration of the imperial museum was held on 5 February 1852. A contemporary of the event, who visited the Hermitage in 1854, recalled: "Of course, we could receive only a general idea, although we walked probably a mile or more across the galleries and halls designed in a luxurious yet austere style. Some of them are allotted to medals and coins... and some others to sculpture, both classical and modern. The largest part is given to paintings..."

In the 1860s the Imperial Museum was opened for the public at large.

The Main Staircase is one of the several interiors in the Winter Palace that give us an idea of the Baroque interiors created by Rastrelli. After the fire of 1837 the staircase was re-created by Vasily Stasov. In the eighteenth century it was known as the Ambassadorial Staircase, because receptions of foreign envoys used to begin at it. Later the staircase had another name – the Jordan Staircase. On Epiphany Day a procession used to descend it and march to the Neva, to the "Jordan" – a pavilion over the hole cut in the ice where the water was consecrated.

The immense space of the staircase, occupying nearly the entire height of the three-storeyed Winter Palace, is filled with light, air and gold shining. Its volumes seem to be even larger thanks to the mirrors mounted in the walls and echoing the shape of the immense windows facing the Neva. The ceiling painted *Olympus,* a work by the eighteenth-century Venetian master Gasparo Diziani, served to enhance the impression. The heavens with figures of ancient gods depicted by the artist seem to unfold the infinity and break the surface of the ceiling through, as it were, producing an impression of endless space.

The Main Staircase branches from the lower landing into two flights of stairs. They make a sharp turn and meet again at the upper landing where a majestic row of granite columns can be seen. The lavish decoration of the walls covered with moulded and gilded ornaments of whimsical design matches this elaborate and dynamic composition.

The statuary in the décor of the staircase has a symbolic message personifying the might and flowering of the Russian State. Among the statues are *Justice* (in the central niche), *Wisdom* and other allegories.

The marble steps of the Jordan Staircase lead to the state halls where imperial receptions, majestic ceremonies and court celebrations were arranged.

**The Main Staircase of the Winter Palace
Architect: Francesco
Bartolomeo Rastrelli. 1754–62**

**Alvise de Tagliapetra (1670–1747)
Justice. Early 18th century. Marble**

interior serves for connecting various sections of the Winter Palace. The doors at its four sides open the way from the Main Staircase in three directions, the principal one of which – through the Field Marshals' and Peter Halls towards the Large Throne Room – is indicated by the columned porticoes set up only at the two of the four doorways.

The Field Marshals' Hall and the neighbouring Peter Hall were created by Montferrand in 1833–34, but less than four years later, in 1837, the great fire broke out here and lasted for more than thirty hours. Probably the principal cause of the tragedy was the order of Nicholas I to carry out a large-scale and toilsome work in a very brief time. Preparing space for the construction of new interiors, builders dismantled the former rooms of the first and second floors and in a hurry did not block with bricks the vent from the flue that later appeared to be at the level of the balcony of the Field Marshals' Hall. This fault, as well as the wide use of wood in the décor and design of the rooms, later led to the catastrophe. The fire broke up in the Field Marshals' Hall and was spreading so quickly that all attempts to save the building proved to be futile. Witnesses described that the glow of the fire could be seen by wayfarers on roads and by peasants in villages some fifty miles from the capital. A company of palace grenadiers and Guards battalions on duty

The Field Marshals' Hall designed by Auguste de Montferrand opens the Great Enfilade of the state rooms of the Winter Palace, running from the Ambassadorial Staircase towards the Large Throne Room. It was here that the court guards, depicted in the watercolour by Eduard Hau (1807–1887), were standing.

The interior owes its name to the formal portraits of the Russian Field Marshals set up in niches at the walls in the nineteenth century. This honour was given only to those among the Field Marshals who were granted honourary additions to their surnames based on the place-names of their outstanding victories: Alexander Suvrov-Rymniksky, Mikhail Kutuzov-Smolensky, Piotr Rumiantsev-Zadunaisky, Grigory Potemkin-Tavrichesky, Ivan Paskevich-Yerivansky, Ivan Diebitsch-Zabalkansky. Portraits were installed only in six of the eight niches in the Field Marshals' Hall – two of them were left blank to encourage army commanders to win the honour of being represented in this hall.

In contrast to the Baroque splendour of the Ambassadorial Staircase, the classical Field Marshals' Hall looks especially austere. The architecture of this interior that served in fact as a setting for the representations of the Field Marshals, is subordinate to its subject matter: the smooth surface of the walls is broken merely by flat twin pilasters not distracting viewers from the portraits in the niches. The columns are employed only in the articulation of the two porticoes, which is also due to the position of the hall. This

were carrying out all they could lift. Marble statues, stone and porcelain vases, paintings, carpets, chests, sofas, books, chandeliers and other precious objects were heaped on the trampled snow in Palace Square.

In order to evade the repetition of the catastrophe, the use of easily flammable wood during the restoration was restricted. The rafters were made of iron, brick vaults replaced the wooden beams and wooden ceiling roofs in large rooms were completely ousted by metal ones. Instead of the stoves that had stood in all rooms before the fire, a system of air heating designed by the engineer N. Ammosov was introduced in the Winter Palace. Fireplaces and stoves began to play mcrcly an auxiliary role.

The Field Marshals' Hall was re-created, like other state interiors, by the architect Vasily Stasov.

Nicolas Sebastien Froste (1790–1856)
Portrait of Alexander Suvorov

Piotr Basin (1793–1877)
Portrait of Mikhail Kutuzov

The Large Field Marshal Hall
Watercolour by Eduard Hau. 1866

The Peter Hall (Small Throne Room), created in 1833–34 by Auguste de Montferrand, is dedicated to the memory of Peter the Great. The deep recess in the eastern wall, between two columns, bears a painting by the Italian artist Jacopo Amiconi. It depicts Peter the Great and Minerva, the ancient goddess of wisdom. The Lyon velvet covering the walls of the hall, is embroidered with silver double-headed eagles. The décor of the interior had a recurrent pattern with the monogram of Peter the Great.

The Peter Hall or the Small Throne Room. Architect: Auguste de Montferrand. 1833–34

Jacopo Amiconi (1675–1752). *Peter the Great and Minerva.* **Between 1732 and 1734**

The Armorial Hall, with an area more than a thousand square metres, is one of the largest in the royal residence. It was created by Vasily Stasov during the restoration of the palace after the fire. Having retained only the former general idea of a hall with columns, Stasov expanded its dimensions and gave a different accent to its architecture. The emphatically monumental character of the Corinthian colonnade and its overall gilding lend to this state interior a feeling of grandeur and somewhat heavy majesty associated with the might of the Russian Empire.

In the second half of the nineteenth and in the early twentieth centuries the rooms of the Great Enfilade were used for ceremonies of majestic processions to the St George Hall

(Large Throne Room), which defined the specific decorative features of each of them. While the memorial Peter Hall was associated with the creator of the Russian Empire, the Armorial Hall illustrated the state system of Russia. The shield decorating the lower tier of the bronze chandeliers, bear representations of the emblems of the Russian provinces. In the nineteenth century the emblems were held on the shafts of spears held by warriors in the sculptural groups near the butt-end walls of the hall.

The Armorial Hall. Architect: Vasily Stasov. 1838–39

Franz von Krüger. *Portrait of Alexander I.* 1837

The 1812 War Gallery. 1812. Architect: Carlo Rossi. 1826

21

The 1812 War Gallery is one of the most famous interiors of the Winter Palace. The ensemble was created to a design by Carlo Rossi, the leading St Petersburg architect of the Empire style. The gallery was conceived as a memorial of history and art devoted to the heroes of the Patriotic War of 1812 and the Russian Army's foreign campaigns of 1813 and 1814. Located directly near the entrance to the Large Throne Room, this interior was to remind to participants in imperial receptions about the martial glory of Russia.

The side wall of the gallery bears the equestrian portrait of Alexander I, a work by the German painter Franz von Krüger (1797–1867). The Emperor is shown mounted, on his horse named Eclipse, presented to him by Napoleon in Erfurt in 1808. The Russian Sovereign used this horse during his solemn entrance to Paris in 1814. Next to the portrait of Alexander I are equestrian portraits of monarchs of the allied states, Frederick William III of Prussia, also a work by Krüger, and the likeness of the Austrian Emperor Francis I by Peter Kraft (1780–1856).

The longer walls of the gallery feature 399 half-length portraits of generals, arranged in five rows. They were executed between 1819 and 1828 by the English painter George Dawe (1781–1829) and his assistants, the St Petersburg artists Alexander Poliakov (1801?–1835) and Vasily Golicke (1802–1848).

In the central section of the gallery one can see Dawe's full-length portraits of the Russian army commanders Mikhail Kutuzov and Mikhail Barclay de Tolly, as well as the English army leader Duke Wellington and the Russian Grand Duke Konstantin Pavlovich.

Mikhail Kutuzov, who headed the Russian Army that defeated Napoleon's army and expelled it from the Russian territory, is depicted standing on an elevation. The portrait is set against a winter landscape, with a depiction of the Russian Army pursuing the French in the background.

A place of honour, near the portraits of Kutuzov and Barclay de Tolly, is given to the depictions of generals, including the likeness of Prince Piotr Bagration, a hero of twenty campaigns and wars and a participant in 150 battles. Napoleon called "the best general of the Russian Army". Bagration was mortally wounded during the Battle of Borodino on 26 August 1812. The remains of the great soldier, who had died on 12 September 1812, were transferred in 1839 to the Field of Borodino.

Over the doors and side walls are moulded laurel wreaths with the names of the places where the most significant battles were held.

The War Gallery was opened in a solemn atmosphere on 25 December 1826 – the day of the annual celebration of "the delivery from the enemy in 1812". Among those present at the ceremony were generals and officers, veterans of the war, as well as soldiers of the guards regiments awarded with medals for the campaigns of 1812–14. In the subsequent years on this day an analogion with the icon of the Saviour was placed opposite the portrait of Alexander I and a religious service was performed in the presence of the war veterans.

During the disastrous fire of 1837 the guard soldiers saved all the portraits. After the fire Vasily Stasov re-created the gallery.

Bagration's close friend was General Nikolai Rayevsky, a hero of battles at Smolensk and Borodino. The outstanding poet Alexander Pushkin, a friend of the entire Rayevsky family, characterized him as "a bright-minded man with a simple and beautiful soul". Denis Davydov, a partisan and poet, who wrote the words "I consider myself to be born solely for the fatal 1812", covered his name with romantic glory.

Not all portraits in the 1812 War Gallery were painted from life. In some cases the earlier likenesses were used as models. This refers primarily to those soldiers who were not alive during the creation of the gallery. For example, the portrait of Piotr Bagration was based from his life-time likeness. Thirteen frames lined with green cloth have always remained blank – they are to remind about the generals whose portraits could not be put in the gallery for some reasons. The frames bear their names and military ranks.

George Dawe
Portrait of Piotr Bagration. **Before 1825**

George Dawe
Portrait of Nikolai Rayevsky. **Before 1828**

George Dawe
Portrait of Denis Davydov. **Before 1828**

George Dawe
Portrait of Mikhail Kutuzov. **1829**

Created by Giacomo Quarenghi in the classical style, the Great Throne Room (St George Hall) was intended for the most important official ceremonies. It was opened in a majestic atmosphere in 1795.

The large (about 800 square metres in area) interior with two tiers of arched windows alternating with doubled Corinthian columns is remarkable for the clarity of proportions characteristic of the work of Giacomo Quarenghi, a brilliant master of Classicism. The architect Vasily Stasov, who re-created the interior after the fire, preserved the overall composition and the structural harmony of the original interior, but also made a number of important alterations. Thus the architectural design of the St George Hall combines the ideas of two architects from different generations.

The ceiling of the hall is made up of copper sheets fixed on a special metal structure. The ornament of the ceiling recurs in the design of the parquet floor inlaid of sixteen different kinds of wood.

The Throne Place is near the side wall. On a dais, under a canopy, stands the wooden throne decorated with silver-gilt plaques. The London craftsman Nicolas Clausen produced it for Anna Ioannovna as early as 1731. Mounted in the wall over the Throne Place is a marble bas-relief depicting the victorious St George, whose name the hall bears.

The Large Throne Room (St George Hall). The Throne Place

**The Large Throne Room (St George Hall). Architect: Giacomo Quarenghi. 1795.
Re-created by Vasily Stasov. 1843**

The Large Church situated near the St George Hall was consecrated in 1762 as the Resurrection Church. Later, in 1763, it was consecrated anew, in honour of the icon of the Vernicle. This is one of the three interiors of the residence that have preserved Rastrelli's initial design. The spatial interior, well lit and abundantly decorated with elaborate moulded and gilded ornaments, is nearly completely devoid of features familiar to Russian devotional architecture before Rastrelli. Stasov, who restored the décor of the interior after the fire of 1837, has retained the overall spirit of Rastrelli's Baroque interior.

The Large Church was intended for religious services on special festive occasions. Thus the wedding of Emperor Nicholas II and Alexandra Fiodorovna (née Princess Alice of Hesse-Darmstadt) took place here on 14 November 1894.

Lauritz Tuxen (1853–1927)
*The Wedding of Nicholas II and Grand Duchess Alexandra Fiodorovna
on 14 (26 O.S.) November 1894.* 1895

The Large Church. Watercolour by Eduard Hau. 1860s

The architect Briullov designed the Alexander Hall during the restoration of the Winter Palace after the fire. An architect of the Historical style, Briullov combined in this interior "Gothic" fan-shaped vaults and bundles of thin columns with gently sloping domes "in the Byzantine taste".

The hall is devoted to the memory of Alexander I. The subject matter of the moulded decoration, densely covering the second tier of the interior, is closely connected with its designation. The décor of the walls and vaults commemorates the War of 1812. The design incorporates enlarged copies of the well-known medals by Fiodor Tolstoy (1783–1873) bearing allegorical representations of the most significant events of the Patriotic War of 1812 and the Russian Army's foreign campaigns of 1813 and 1814.

The Alexander Hall
Details of moulded décor

The Alexander Hall
Architect: Alexander Briullov. 1838–39

The suite of rooms of the palace overlooking Palace Square is used to display French art of the fifteenth to eighteenth century. The rooms located to the east of the Alexander Hall are devoted to works by masters of the eighteenth century – the age when France played the leading role in European culture. One of the exhibits is the statue *Cupid*. The image of the ancient god of love, coquettish and sly, was created by the sculptor Etienne Maurice Falconet (1716–1791), the designer of the St Petersburg monument to Peter the Great known generally as the "Bronze Horseman".

Hall of Eighteenth-Century French Art (The Cupid Hall).
Architect: Alexander Briullov. *Ca* **1840**

Etienne Maurice Falconet. *Cupid.* **1750s. Marble**

Jean-Baptiste Siméon Chardin
A Washerwoman. **1730s**

Jean-Baptiste Siméon Chardin
Still Life with the Attributes of the Arts. **1766**

One can also see here paintings by the most outstanding artists of the century. *A Washerwoman* by Jean-Baptiste Siméon Chardin (1699–1779) is a fine example of genre painting that made this major master of the Age of Enlightenment especially popular. The charm of everyday scene lies in its intimate poetic mood. A significant place in Chardin's work belonged to still-life painting. The artist painted for the Russian Empress Catherine the Great *Still Life with the Attributes of the Arts,* where the palette and brushes symbolize painting, the figure of Mercury (a work by the sculptor Jean-Baptiste Pigalle) alludes to sculpture and drawing and drawing instruments refer to architecture. A master of complex colouring rich in nuances and free, energetic brushstrokes, Chardin inherited the traditions of the great colourist Antoine Watteau (1684–1721).

A subtle lyric, Antoine Watteau created in painting a specific new genre that was defined by his contemporaries as *scènes galantes*. One of such works is *The Capricious Woman,* a canvas executed in the artist's characteristic manner: small divided brushstrokes form the vibrant texture of the canvas and its colour gamut is woven of the most elaborate chromatic shades. A mild humour, with which the characters of this "gallant scene" are represented, is combined with a sad, elegiac dreaminess typical of emotional atmosphere of Watteau's works.

The decorative and idyllic *Landscape in the Environs of Beauvais* by François Boucher (1703–1770) acquaints us with a favourite motif and manner of one of the most popular masters of Rococo art. Echoes of this refined style are still sensible in the work of Boucher's younger contemporary – Jean Honoré Fragonard (1732–1808), whose creative career ended in the subsequent century. They can be noticed in the gracious composition *A Stolen Kiss* that allows one to appreciate the virtuosity of the artist's brilliant brushwork.

Antoine Watteau. ***The Capricious Woman.*** **1718**

Jean Honoré Fragonard. ***A Stolen Kiss.*** **Second half of the 1780s**

François Boucher. ***Landscape in the Environs of Beauvais.*** **Early 1740s**

Antoine Jean Gros. *Napoleon Bonaparte on the Bridge at Arcole.* 1796–97

Jacques Louis Davis. *Sappho and Phaon.* 1809

The rooms of the second floor in the southern section of the palace house the display of French art of the nineteenth and twentieth centuries – the period when innovatory trends that shaped the character of European artistic life emerged in France. The represented works that belong to the treasury of world culture introduce visitors to these trends.

The canvas *Sappho and Phaon* was created by Jacques Louis David (1740–1825), the head of Neo-Classicism, a movement that turned to the traditions of Classical Antiquity and Italian Renaissance. The main character of the painting is the famous ancient Greek poetess Sappho, who fell in love, according to a legend, with the youth Phaon and killed herself when her lover grew cold to her. The figure of Cupid handing over a lyre to Sappho reminds us that the poetess is famous for her love lyrics. The two trees in the landscape and the kissing doves are symbols of love. The clarity of the closed composition, the sculptural forms and the clear-cut design are the features of the austere classical idiom.

One of David's most gifted pupils, Antoine Jean Gros (1771–1835) created a vivid character of the contemporary hero in his painting *Napoleon Bonaparte on the Bridge at Arcole,* combining the elements of portraiture and historical painting in it. The work is based on the episode from the history of the Italian Campaign undertaken in 1796 by the French army under the command of the future Emperor of France. Fighting with the Austrians at Arcole, Napoleon brought soldiers to the bridge giving them a lead under the enemy's fire and thus won the battle. The structural balance in the canvas, the generalized figure of its protagonist and the sculptural plasticity of his face suggest Gros's tribute to the artistic principles of David. However, the "fragmentary" composition of the painting, a certain agitation of its colour range and the mobility of its texture foresee the devices of the forthcoming Romantic painting.

François Gérard (1770–1837), the creator of the formal *Portrait of Josephine,* also was David's pupil. The consort of Napoleon, then the First Consul of the French Republic, is represented on the park terrace of her Malmaison castle. The first lady of France has a dress and hairstyle in the "Greek" taste characteristic of that age. The impressive monumental work combines a representative character with poetic intonations. Its emotional atmosphere betrays some echoes of Sentimentalism – a literary and artistic trend of the past century, as well as a response to new art movements.

Portrait of Count Nikolai Guryev is a first-rate example of this genre in the work of Jacques Dominique Ingres (1780–1867), David's best pupil and the most prominent artist of his time. The painter produced this portrait of the Russian aristocrat, who served as a diplomat, in Florence. The significance of the created image is combined with its indubitable authenticity in the rendering of the sitter's appearance. The concise idiom of Neo Classicism, a staunch champion of principles of which Ingres was, is recognizable in the sculpture-like clarity of generalized forms, in the austere rhythm of pure lines and in the manner of setting the monumental figure in the rectangle of the canvas. At the same time the inner tension observed in the Count's face and the dull sky in the background introduce a dramatic touch to the mood of the painting, suggesting its link, independently of Ingres's will, to works by the Romanticists.

Contemporaries gave to the young generation of artists, who sought to express their individual world perception and personal feelings, the name of the Romantic generation. One of regular sources of inspiration of the Romantics was the mysterious, colourful and exotic East. *A Moroccan Saddling a Horse* by Eugène Delacroix (1798–1863), a leader of the Romantic movement in painting, is not merely a scene reflecting the master's Moroccan impressions. It is the image of a free world reigned by the spirit of man's natural ease and unconstraint. The work owes its agitated pathetic element to the energetic contrasts of colour, changing illumination, dynamic linear design and vigorous brushwork.

Eugène Delacroix
A Moroccan Saddling a Horse. 1855

Jean Dominique Ingres
Portrait of Count Nikolai Guryev. 1821

François Gérard. ***Portrait of Josephine.*** 1801

The display introduces visitors not only to the work of innovatory artists, but to those masters who relied on the aesthetic norms established by the Academy of Arts, too. This kind of art, accessible to the official Paris salons and chosen by members of the Academy for them in keeping with its demands, became known as Salon art. The type of the formal society portrait characteristic of the Salon was created by François Xavier Winterhalter (1805–1873). The portrait painter to the court of the French monarchs, active also for the Prussian and English royal houses, he painted many representatives of the Russian aristocracy and members of the family of the Russian Sovereigns. His *Portrait of Grand Duchess Maria Nikolayevna,* daughter of Nicholas I, belongs to this kind of works.

Subjects from the life of Ancient Greece and Rome took a prominent place among favourite themes of Academic painters. Such motifs often inspired the once well-known representative of official art Jean-Léon Gérôme (1824–1904). His painting *The Sale of a Slave Girl* depicts an episode at a slave market in Rome. Gérôme treated this intimate, bright-coloured canvas, as it was typical for a Salon master, not so much in a dramatic vein as in the spirit of an entertaining genre scene with a tinge of exoticism.

The 1830s saw the emergence of Realism, a trend whose adherents turned directly to nature and engaged in a desperate struggle with the official tradition.

François Xavier Winterhalter
Portrait of Grand Duchess Maria Nikolayevna. 1857

Jean-Léon Gérôme. *The Sale of a Slave Girl. Ca* 1884

Landscape occupies a prominent place in the art of Realist artists. This kind of painting is associated mainly with the work of the Barbizon group – the painters who settled, in search of natural motifs, in the village of Barbizon, near the Forest of Fontainebleau. *A Market in Normandy,* a small painting by Théodore Rousseau (1812–1867), the leader of the Barbizon school, was inspired by the master's trip to Normandy. Capturing the unassuming motif without preconceived ideas or idealization, Rousseau subtly rendered the specific poetry of quiet provincial life and the charm of an early morning.

The large-scale canvas *Setting Off for Market* ranks with the most famous works by Constant Troyon (1810–1865), a landscape and animal painter close to the circle of the Barbizon painters. A herd of cows in a country setting was the favourite theme of this painter nicknamed the "Rembrandt of cows" as his works reminded to his contemporaries of the subjects favoured by seventeenth-century Dutch masters.

Camille Corot (1796–1875), an artist with a distinct lyrical and Romantic perception of nature, occupies a place apart in landscape painting. His intimate, elegiac canvases, treated in the subtlest shades of greyish-pearly tone, convey the atmosphere in which all the shapes appear vague and the outlines seem to dissolve.

Théodore Rousseau. *A Market in Normandy.* 1830s

Jean-Baptiste Camille Corot. *Peasant Woman Pasturing a Cow by the Edge of a Forest.* 1865–1870s

Constant Troyon. *Setting Off for Market.* 1859

Realism paved the way for those artists who set the task of capturing the immediate, fleeting impressions of nature. Having abandoned their studios, they began to paint *en plein air*, out of doors, so as to arrest on the canvas the passing moment of the ever-changing world. Works by these masters were called, at first in derision, as Impressionism, from the French word *impression*. Claude Monet (1840–1926), who united the Impressionists, worked mainly in the field of landscape painting. The picture *Ladies in the Garden at Sainte-Addresse,* created near Le Havre, on the estate of the artist's relations, dates from the initial period of Impressionism, but he already chose sunlight as its motif. And it is on light effects that Monet and his Impressionist friends would focus their efforts later. Creating this painting directly from life, the master developed a system of colour gradations depending on lighting.

Monet's *Corner of the Garden at Montgeron* demonstrates the mature phase in the development of the Impressionist method. The artist's brush vividly conveyed the lavishly flowering garden and the atmosphere that seems to dissolve the forms and silhouettes. The impression "caught" by the painter's eye is realized on the canvas in a "sketchy" manner, with a divided brushstroke that promotes the optic mixture of colours thus ensuring the painting's chromatic purity and saturation with light. The "fragmentary" composition of the picture is also characteristic of Impressionism. Monet chose as the motif of the decorative panel executed for the banker Hochédé, the owner of the Montgeron estate near Paris, a corner of the garden surrounding the estate mansion. The Hermitage also owns its companion painting, *The Pond at Montgeron.*

Poppy Field is one of Monet's numerous intimate works painted in the environs of Giverny, a country place where he lived for forty years and was buried according to his will.

Claude Monet. *Ladies in the Garden at Sainte-Addresse.* 1867

Claude Monet. *Corner of the Garden at Montgeron.* 1876

Claude Monet. *Poppy Field.* 1887

Portraiture was the main genre in the work of Auguste Renoir (1841–1919). *Portrait of the Actress Jeanne Samary* is one of his most famous works. The artist painted this young and charming Parisian woman, an actress of the famous French Theatre ("Comédie Française"), several times. Many years later Renoir recalled the actress, who had prematurely died, in his conversations with his son: "What a charming girl! And what skin! She was all literally shining." This portrait differs from his half-length, intimate depictions of Jeanne by its large dimensions and a somewhat representative quality – Renoir was preparing for the Salon of 1879 that became a crucial moment in his fight for recognition. Nevertheless following the Impressionist principle of reflecting natural life, Renoir presented the actress in her accustomed setting of a society salon or a theatrical foyer. The subtle colour nuances render the shining of her golden hair, her matt skin and the light foam of lace, vibrant with colour, on her dress.

Girl with a Fan is a portrait of Alphonsine Fournaise, daughter of a restaurant owner at Chatou, in the environs of Paris where the Impressionists often worked.

Depicting the "beautiful Alphonsine", as the girl was commonly called in the restaurant of her father, Renoir captured the vivid glitter of her eyes and her fleeting glance. The model that delighted the artist by her youthful charm and freshness belongs to the "Renoir" type of women.

The image of a "Renoir"-type child, attractive and touchingly unconstrained, was created by the master in his painting *Child with a Whip*. The portrait of the five-year-old Etienne Goujon, wearing a dress according to the fashion of that period, conveys the natural grace of the childish appearance. The distinct line shaping the boy's face reminds us that in that period Renoir sought to attain the classical purity of drawing in the spirit of Raphael and Ingres (this manner became known as the "Ingres" or "rigid" style). At the same time the artist uses a free sweeping manner to render the reflexes of sunlight on the sand avenue, the verdure of the park skirting it and the light dress with colour reflexes playing on it. Renoir painted this portrait as a commission of Senator Goujon, the boy's father.

Pierre Auguste Renoir
***Portrait of the Actress Jeanne Samary.* 1878**

Pierre Auguste Renoir. *Girl with a Fan.* 1881

Pierre Auguste Renoir. *Child with a Whip.* 1885

The canvas *Windy Day at Veneux* gives an idea of the mature manner of Alfred Sisley (1839–1899), a landscape painter endowed with emotional keenness and lyrical penetration. The unassuming motif implements the living breath of nature. The dull weather has not made it colourless – the grey-green tonality is iridescent with chromatic tints vibrating in the light that dissolves in the atmosphere. The mobile and diverse brushstrokes skillfully convey the movement of air torrents following their directions.

The townscape played a significant role in the work of Camille Pissarro (1830–1903). His *Boulevard Montmartre* in Paris is an example from a whole series of canvases featuring this Parisian boulevard with its changing atmosphere and conveying the pulsation of its intense, never ceasing life. The painter's dynamic and precise brushwork corresponds to its tempo and rhythm. Edgar Degas (1834–1917), who also tried to capture "moments in life", depicted in his pastel *Woman Combing Her Hair* a scene that seems to be observed, as it were, "through a keyhole", as the artist himself expressed it. The charm of the commonplace episode lies in the woman's ease of posture, in the natural plasticity of her naked body and in her convincing gestures and movements.

Alfred Sisley. *Windy Day at Veneux.* **1882**

Camille Pissarro. *Boulevard Montmartre in Paris.* **1897**

Edgar Degas. *Woman Combing Her Hair. Ca* **1885**

Paul Cézanne. *The Smoker. Ca* 1890–92

Paul Cézanne. *Still Life with Drapery. Ca* 1894–95

The last decades of the nineteenth century saw the formation of diverse new artistic phenomena, united by the general conventional term of Post-Impressionism, a trend based on the mastery of Impressionism and yet opposing to it novel artistic developments. Each representative of this trend created the artistic idiom of his own in order to express in art his personal vision of the world. Thus, Paul Cézanne (1839–1906), unlike his Impressionist friends, who depicted the ever-changing world, conveyed by means of painting an idea of the everlasting values of the universe and its eternal laws. Cézanne's *Smoker* belongs to a series of his paintings showing smokers and card players, which are related to the characters of the Old Masters from the seventeenth century onwards. Cézanne's canvases, however, are devoid of a narrative quality or allegorical message. His smoker, whose monumental figure bespeaks a sort of grandeur, seems to dwell beyond the hustle and bustle of everyday life and to personify an absolute calm and the organic integrity of nature. This image is reminiscent of Cézanne's words "I like most the appearance of the people who grew old without breaking customs."

Still Life with Drapery is one of Cézanne's most outstanding works in the genre that occupied a prominent place in his creative career. The motif of this picture is similar to those painted by artists in the past ages, but unlike his predecessors, Cézanne does not reveal the textural qualities of different objects. He regards any of them primarily as an implementation of a clear, monolithic plastic form. Having moulded each of these forms by vibrant, pure colours, the master completes it by a blue outline, resembling condensed air. The volumes shown from different points of view appear as parts of a single coherent structure, stable in harmony. The outstanding Austrian poet Rainer Maria Rilke, who was greatly impressed by Cézanne's painting, told about his still lifes that "he made them express the Universe".

The outstanding self-taught artist Vincent van Gogh (1853–1890), who opened for himself in Impressionism the possibilities of pure colours and divided brushstrokes, expressed then his powerful dramatic temperament in the heightened expressiveness of his colour range, in the turbulent energy of his treatment and in the maximally intense texture. In the painting *Remembrance of the Garden at Etten (The Ladies of Arles)* Vincent van Gogh merged his impressions from the bright nature of southern France saturated with sunshine and recollections of his parents' home in the Dutch town of Saint Etten. The female images tinged with melancholy suggest the features of his mother, sister and cousin.

The Lilac Bush is one of Van Gogh's best later works. Staying in the hospital for mental patients at Saint-Rémy, he painted a bush of lilacs growing in the hospital garden. The rapidly growing bush personifies the life-giving power of nature. The agitated resonance of colours and the mobility of the entire mass of brushstrokes create a powerful dramatic tension.

Vincent van Gogh created the painting *Cottages* at Auvers shortly before his death. The great emotional strain used to convey a modest scene of cottages with straw roofs, betrays the uneasy state of the artist's soul.

Vincent van Gogh. *Remembrance of the Garden at Etten (The Ladies of Arles).* 1888

Vincent van Gogh. *Lilac Bush.* 1889

Vincent van Gogh. *Cottages.* 1890

Paul Gauguin (1848–1903) was, like Vincent van Gogh, a self-taught artist, who found his sense of life in painting. Driven by a romantic dream about the world that had preserved its primordial harmony, he left Paris for Polynesia. An image of this dream world conjured up by the master's imagination under the impression of exotic Oceania with its mysterious customs and beliefs, was rendered in the painting *Tahitian Pastorals* on Tahiti Island. The pastoral, an idyllic scene of shepherds' life, had emerged as a genre in French art in the Rococo age. Gauguin represented in this work an idyll of the "primordial" life of the island's inhabitants. The action depicted here takes place in the evening – the time of music and ritual dances of the aborigines in honour of the goddess of the Moon. The heightened intensity of colouring, the prevalence of surface over space, the rhythm of the linear design and generalized colour spots – all these expressive means are used to heighten the decorative effect of the composition. The same manner, characteristic of Gauguin's Tahitian period, is employed in his *Woman Holding a Fruit*. The primeval rhythm of life dominates the everyday scene. The Tahitian woman with a fruit shown in the forefront is the veritable "Eva" of this aboriginal paradise with its eternal accord between man and nature.

Paul Gauguin. *Tahitian Pastorals*. 1892

Paul Gauguin. *Woman Holding a Fruit*. 1893

New radical trends in French art of the early twentieth century are associated mainly with the two great masters – Pablo Picasso (1881–1973) and Henri Matisse (1869–1954). *The Absinthe Drinker,* created by Picasso at the age of twenty, is done with an uncompromising boldness. The sharply distorted proportions of the flattened body, contrasting with the face-skull and the huge bony arms, the intense colour gamut – these are the concise means which are used to create a tragic image of a drunkard who came to a deadlock of solitude. *Guitar and Violin* belongs to so-called Synthetic Cubism. Revealing the fundamental structures of the world, the painter simplified and generalized geometrical forms. From recognizable fragments of material objects he created a composition dominated by strict logic and clear rhythm.

Pablo Picasso. *The Absinthe Drinker.* 1901

Pablo Picasso. *Woman with a Fan.* 1907

Pablo Picasso. *Guitar and Violin. Ca* 1912

While Picasso discovered new possibilities in the world of plastic forms, the discoveries of Henri Matisse belonged to the field of colour treatment. As the artist declared, "there must appear in the painting an accord of colours – a harmony similar to musical harmony." Matisse attained such "accord of colours" in his decorative panel *The Red Room* that is also known as *Harmony in Red*. The artist's will and his feel for colour have transformed an everyday scene taken from life – a dining room with a décor usual for this kind of interior. The arabesque motifs of the ornament, underlining the entire flattened space of the painting, set the rhythm that dominates the silhouette of the woman laying the table, the outlines of trees behind the windows and the lines skirting fruit, vases and carafes.

"Colours act stronger when they are simpler and the impact of heightened colour is like the strike of a gong," told Matisse. A convincing proof of the artist's rightness are his companion panels *The Dance* and *Music,* in which a juxtaposition of several ultimately saturated colours not only creates a powerful decorative effect but provides a meaningful associative and emotional impact. The expressiveness of *The Dance* with its outburst of unrestrained movement of huge female figures contrasts with the calm and clarity of *Music*, a canvas in which the static figurines of seated singing boys are reminiscent of a sheet of music, while the standing violinist reminds us of treble clef. Both panels, ranking with Matisse's most monumental canvases of this period, were intended for the staircase of the Moscow mansion of Sergei Shchukin, his first art patron and one of the first Russian collectors of new French painting.

Henri Matisse. *The Red Room (Harmony in Red).* 1908

Henri Matisse. *Music.* 1910

Henri Matisse. *The Dance.* 1910

Auguste Rodin. *The Poet and the Muse* (in the background). *Ca* 1905. Marble

Auguste Rodin. *Romeo and Juliet.* 1905. Marble

Auguste Rodin. *Eternal Spring.* Early 1900s. Marble

A notion about Impressionism in the art of sculpture is associated with Auguste Rodin (1840–1917), a major sculptor of his age. His small-scale works, such as the most popular *Eternal Spring* or *Romeo and Juliet,* inspired by Shakespeare's great tragedy, implement the poetry of eternal and ever beautiful feeling. The images of his sculpture *The Poet and the Muse* seem to personify the nature of creativity based on imagination and love. Literary and symbolic motifs are combined in his works with an Impressionist treatment of plastic form that is revealed in the vague and fluent "incompleteness" of volumes and lines and in a special soft, "airy" quality of his texture.

The small canvases *Winter Landscape* and *View in Murnau* by Wassily Kandinsky (1866–1944), a painter of Russian descent active in Germany and France, remind us by their bright colours, lavishly applied on to the canvas, the artist's words: "I liked colours most of all." Kandinsky took a decision to devote himself to painting at the age of thirteen and studied under famous masters in the celebrated schools of Germany, with which his basic creative career was later associated. In 1911 he organized in Munich the Blaue Reiter art union that entered the history of art as a society of Expressionist artists, whose works are characterized by the heightened expressiveness of colour. Kandinsky won a worldwide fame, however, primarily as a founder of Abstractionism. The large-scale canvas *Composition VI*, created two years after he had produced his first abstract work (in the medium of watercolour), is one of the ten monumental programmatic paintings called "compositions" by the master himself. It was in these works that Kandinsky most fully expressed his conviction that art "should serve development and improvement of man's soul, should speak to the soul about its daily bread." The main idea implemented in the *Composition* is a transformation of the world: from chaos, through crisis, to a new harmony.

Wassily Kandinsky. *Winter Landscape.* 1909

Wassily Kandinsky. *View of Murnau.* 1908

Wassily Kandinsky. *Composition VI.* 1913

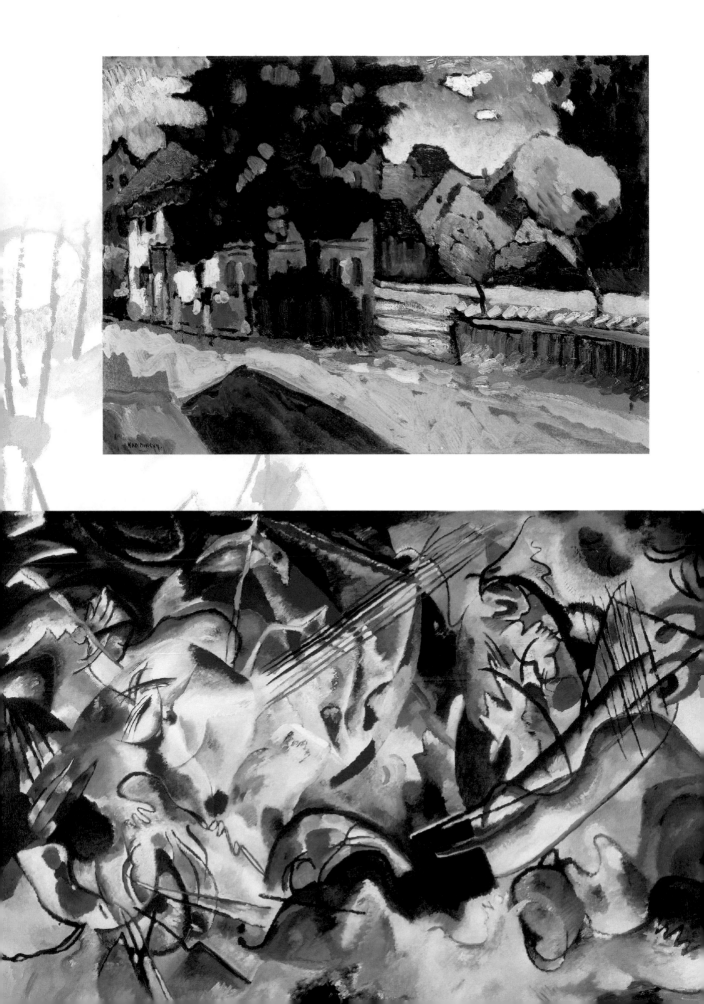

The White Hall, with its décor sustained in a white colour, was created by Alexander Briullov after a fire in the palace. A connoisseur of art of previous periods, the architect designed this interior in the traditions of ancient Roman architecture. The monumental forms, the powerful vault with two resilient arches, the majestic rhythm of the Corinthian columns and pilasters, all contributes to the majestic appearance of this hall filled with light and air. The décor is dominated by ancient motifs, the walls are embellished with bas-reliefs representing Olympic gods and the moulded design includes elements of ancient ornamentation. The frieze in the upper part of the walls is embellished with the figurines of *putti* engaged in various arts and crafts. The statues under the columns symbolize Architecture, Sculpture, Painting and Music. The fireplace trimmed with dark marble, the mahogany doors and the ormolu candlesticks introduce impressive accents into the colour range of the hall.

The richly decorated White Hall completed the apartments of the Crown Prince, the future Emperor Alexander II, and his consort. Today it contains a part of the display of French art of the eighteenth century – canvases by Hubert Robert (1733–1808) and other painters, the famous Sèvres porcelain ware and furniture by David Roentgen (1743–1807).

The White Hall. Architect: Alexander Briullov. 1841

The White Hall. Part of the display of eighteenth-century French art

Immediately behind the White Hall, in the south-western projection of the Winter Palace, is the Gold Drawing Room. Like the White Hall, it was created by Alexander Briullov in the apartments of the heir to the throne (the future Emperor Alexander II), for his wedding that was held in April 1841.

The name "apartments" was traditionally applied in the Winter Palace to the groups of rooms united by their general designation and belonging to a single owner. Thus, after the fire eight living apartments were formed in the Winter Palace. Among them were those of the heir provided with a separate entrance from Palace Square and including the private apartments of the Tsesarevich, the rooms of his future consort Maria Alexandrovna (née Princess of Hesse-Darmstadt) and two official halls, the Gold Drawing Room and the White Hall.

The Gold Drawing Room owes its name to the abundance of gold in its decoration. The walls and pylons are gilded all over and the rather low cylindrical vaults are covered with moulded and gilded ornaments running along the white background.

In the 1850s the décor of the drawing room was somewhat altered by Andrei Stackenschneider; some alterations were also undertaken later. Originally only the light ornament in all sections of the hall was gilded and the all-over gilding of the walls appeared evidently in the late 1860s or in the 1870s, and it is know that the architect Vladimir Schreiber (1817–1900) participated in the decoration.

A notable element in the décor of the drawing room is an impressive fireplace faced with white marble and embellished with a mosaic panel depicting ancient ruins.

Today, the Gold Drawing Room houses a temporary display entitled "The Fate of a Single Collection: Five Hundred Gems from the Cabinet of the Duke of Orleans". Empress Catherine the Great, a passionate lover of carved stones calling her passion for gems "a stone disease", acquired this collection amassed by the Dukes of Orleans in 1787.

The Gold Drawing Room. Detail of the decor

The Gold Drawing Room
Architects: Alexander Briullov, Andrei Stackenschneider, Victor Schreiber. 19th century

The Gold Drawing Room adjoins the private apartments of Maria Alexandrovna, consort of the heir and later Emperor Alexander II. Her monogram with the interlacing letters M and A is incorporated in the design of the room. It can be seen, for instance, in the Crimson Study over the mirror. Created by Andrei Stackenschneider in 1863, the Crimson Study served for performing music as is suggested by the design of the fabric used in its trimming (a medallion with sheets of music and musical instruments).

The Boudoir, following the Crimson Study, was designed by the architect Harald Bosse in the style of the Second Rococo in 1853. The mirrors mounted not only in the walls, but in the ceiling, too, the carved and gilded frames, the French garnet-coloured fabric lining the walls and furniture, richly adorn this room that was favoured by the Empress, as witnessed by her contemporaries.

The Boudoir. Architect: Harald Bosse. 1853

The Boudoir. Detail of the décor

**The Crimson Study.
Architect: Andrei Stackenschneider. 1863**

PELLE · CVPIDINEOS · TOTO
NE · TVA · POSSIDEAT

CONAMINE · LVXVS
PECTORA · CECA · VENVS

Paintings by Lucas Cranach the Elder (1472–1553) rank with the most significant works in the display of German art of the fifteenth to eighteenth century that occupies several halls in the Winter Palace. The famous artist of the German Renaissance is represented by paintings of different genres. *Venus and Cupid* occupies a distinguished place not only in Cranach's art but in the entire art of Northern Europe. The painting was the earliest depiction of the nude ancient goddess of beauty in the Transalpine countries. Initiated into Humanistic culture, Cranach often turned to ancient subjects, but he interpreted them in accordance with the national artistic tradition, not infrequently accompanying his painted images with edifying inscriptions. Thus he portrayed the beautiful deity as a mysterious tempter dangerous for a virtue. The moral inscription in Latin on the painting reminds us about that: *Drive off Cupid's venery with all your might, lest Venus gain possession of your blinded heart (Pelle Cupideneos toto conamine luxus / Ne tua possideat pectora ceca Venus).* The elongated proportions of the goddess's body, the neutral background, the conventional support for the figures formed by a strip of stony land are the features naturally inherited by the German Renaissance from the Gothic style of the preceding period and simultaneously anticipating the specific artistic language of forthcoming Mannerist art. The painting, one of Cranach's best, is also remarkable for its laconic and still effective and harmonious colour solution.

The *Virgin and Child under the Apple Tree* is a masterpiece of Lucas Cranach's religious painting. The picture is saturated with symbols: the apple-tree alludes to the Tree of Paradise, the apple in the hands of the Infant Christ reminds us about the fall of Adam and Eva redeemed by Christ. The beautiful gold-haired Mary personifies Cranach's ideal of female beauty, which combines the type of the Gothic Virgins, the appearance of fairy-tale princesses and the features of aristocratic ladies, whose portraits Cranach painted at the court of the Saxonian princes. The landscape inspired by the nature of Germany also betrays the fantastic spirit inherent in entire German art of the age of Cranach and characteristic of the work of this painter, too.

Lucas Cranach the Elder. *Venus and Cupid.* **1509**

Lucas Cranach the Elder
The Virgin and Child under the Apple Tree. Ca 1530

Thomas Gainsborough. *Portrait of a Lady in Blue.* Late 1770s – early 1780s

Joseph Wright of Derby. *An Iron Forge Viewed from Without.* 1773

Joshua Reynolds. *Cupid Untying the Zone of Venus.* 1788

The display of English art of the sixteenth to nineteenth century contains works by two major artists of the eighteenth century. *Portrait of a Lady in Blue* is a veritable masterpiece by Thomas Gainsborough (1727–1788), one of the most prominent European portrait painters. The high fashionable hairdo and the deep décolleté of the lady's dress suggest her aristocratic descent and are intended to lend a formal quality to this intimate portrait, but the impressive costume highlights the young woman's charm even more. A special mood of this canvas pervaded with lyricism and spirituality, is largely due to the exquisite grey-blue colour range and a light, virtuoso manner of painting.

The picture *Cupid Untying the Zone of Venus* by Joshua Reynolds (1723–1792), the first President of the English Academy of Arts, is sustained in the optimistic, sonorous colour scheme. The image of a sly goddess with a charming smile was so popular with Reynolds's contemporaries that he repeated this composition several times.

The painting *An Iron Forge Viewed from Without* by Joseph Wright of Derby (1734–1797) depicts a smithy by night. The artist with a romantic sense of the world saw in the night forge a mysterious, fantastic sight, which he conveyed with an expressive emotionality.

◄ **The Malachite Room. Architect: Alexander Briullov. 1839**

The Malachite Room. Part of the display

The Malachite Room. Malachite articles

The Malachite Room is one of the most ornate interiors of the palace. Alexander Briullov created it by the end of the 1830s as a formal drawing room in the apartments of Empress Alexandra Fiodorovna, Nicholas I's consort. The interior owes its name to malachite, a semi-precious stone brought from the Urals and used to adorn the columns pilasters and fireplaces. In the eighteenth century this mineral was a great rarity and it was employed merely for the manufacture of table decorations, writing sets and vases. With the discovery of unusually rich deposits of malachite in the Demidovs' mine in the Urals in the 1830s it became possible to use this stone in interior décor.

Thin plaques of malachite, skillfully selected by stonecutters so as to preserve its natural patterns, were fixed by special sticky mastic on to the base of metal or simple stone. The surface of the article was carefully ground and polished. The same techniques were used in the manufacture of tables, vases and candlesticks thus adding to the magnificent decoration of this hall.

Malachite is especially effective against the white walls, in combination with the overall gilding of the doors, column capitals and gilded pattern of the ceiling.

The Small Dining Room and the Library are two well-preserved interiors of the royal residence designed in the reign of Nicholas II. The rooms allotted in early 1894 to the heir, who became the Emperor in the same year, were decorated under the supervision of Alexander Krasovsky (1848–1923) in the historical style characterized by borrowings from art of different ages. Thus the architect designed the Small Dining Room in the Rococo style, while the décor of the Library goes down to medieval Gothic architecture.

The Small Dining Room served for the imperial family as the place for meals in a narrow domestic circle. The small interior overlooking the inner courtyard by its windows is treated in light, pearl-grey tones. The walls are adorned with tapestries (woven pileless carpets) produced at the St Petersburg Tapestry Factory (three of them depict in an allegorical form the parts of the world: Asia, Africa and America). A moulded ornament with characteristic Rococo motifs (sea-shells, scrolls and garlands) skirts the carpets and runs all along the smooth surfaces of the walls and doors.

The Library of Nicholas I is decorated with the use of two main materials – dark wood and red skin stamped with gold. The motifs of Gothic ornament (pointed arches, pierced trefoils, four-blade rosettes, etc. adorn the book shelved located in two tiers, the railings of the staircase, the parapet of the balcony, the marble fireplace, the ceiling and the windows. The articulation of space is wholly subordinated to the designation of the interior.

The Small Dining Room.
Architect: Alexander Krasovsky. 1894

The Library.
Architect: Alexander Krasovsky. 1894

The Small Dining Room. Clock. France. 18th century

The exhibitions of the Department of the History of Russian Culture occupy more than thirty rooms and halls of the Winter Palace. The most interesting part of the collection of the Russian Department is the assemblage of medieval icons, which includes, along-side works from such major art centres as Novgorod, Pskov and Moscow, a large number of icons painted in the Russian North. This collection was formed large-ly as a result of expeditions organized for collecting works of art. In the 1950s and 1960s the Hermitage researchers investigated many regions in the Russian North. They took icons having artistic value from then non-functioning churches and chapels. Many of icons were thus saved, as they needed restoration. *The Almighty Saviour* (13th–14th century) is one of the earliest exhibits found in the North. It seems that this unusual icon had once been a part of the iconos-tasis in a small village church. Icons were painted in the North not only by professional icon-painters, but also by church sextons, monks of small monasteries and sometimes by peasants. *The Almighty Saviour* is a work by a northern provincial master. It is amaz-ing that the simplicity of devices does not diminish the significance of the iconic image characterized by a quiet and restrained force.

The expedition to the Northern Dvina, organized in 1958, yielded to the Hermitage a large icon, *St Ni-cholas with Scenes from His Life,* datable to the first half of the sixteenth century. This work was created either by a northern master well acquainted with the art of Novgorod or by a Novgorodian painter. The central image of St Nicholas is surrounded with twenty-eight scenes depicting episodes from his life. A large number of the scenes show a tendency to narration characteristic of the sixteenth century.

The icon *St John the Theologian in Silence* was painted in 1679 by Nektary Kuliuksin, a monk of the Kirillo-Belozersky Monastery and donated by him to the church "for the memory of his soul" as is written on the back. The clear rounded lines shaping the fig-ure of St John the Theologian, the careful treatment of the face and clothing testify to the high professional skill of the icon-painter. Nevertheless the style of exe-cution suggests that the seventeenth century marked the end of the Middle Ages in Russia.

Icon: *St Nicholas with Scenes from His Life*
First half of the 16th century

Icon: *The Almighty Saviour*
Second half of the 13th – 14th century

Nektary Kuliuksin.
Icon: *St John the Theologian in Silence.* 1679

The two suites of state rooms in the western part of the Winter Palace house the display of eighteenth-century Russian culture. They reflect both artistic and historical processes that occurred in Russia in the eighteenth century. Works of painting, sculpture, graphic and applied art as well as lathes and tools of the period illustrate the age of reforms initiated by Peter the Great.

One of the halls is used to display exhibits giving an idea about the character of interiors in Peter's age, when furniture of different countries and styles was combined. The oval extension table with unfolding leaves was created by Arkhangelsk craftsmen from an English example. Imitating an inlaid ornament of various kinds of wood, Russian craftsmen painted the table-top with tem-

**Russian Culture of the First Half
of the Eighteenth Century. Part of the display**

**Ivan Vishniakov
Portrait of Stepanida Yakovleva. After 1756**

**Alexei Antropov
Portrait of Father Fiodor Dubiansky. 1761**

**Russian Culture of the Second Half
of the Eighteenth Century. Part of the display**

pera pigments in the traditional technique of icon-painting. On the wall is a carpet depicting the Battle of Poltava. This is one of the earliest Russian tapestries woven in 1722 at the factory founded by Peter the Great.

Russian painting of the mid-eighteenth century is represented in the Hermitage basically by portraits. Among portrait painters active in that period were such eminent masters as Ivan Vishniakov (1699–1761) and Alexei Antropov (1716–1795). Vishniakov painted a formal portrait of the young merchant woman Stepanida Yakovleva, commissioned from the artist for her wedding. Antropov created the likeness of Father Fiodor Dubiansky, the spiritual father of Empress Elizabeth, treating the sitter as a man of great spiritual strength.

In one of the display rooms devoted to the culture of the second half of the eighteenth century, visitors can see the throne of the Grand Master of the Maltese Order. It was created from a drawing by Giacomo Quarenghi for Paul I, who was proclaimed the Grand Master of the order in 1798. Displayed here is also the large tapestry *Hector Reproaching Paris,* based on Homer's *Iliad* and woven at the St Petersburg Tapestry Manufactory in 1773.

81

When the imperial royal residence was being converted into a museum building, some auxiliary rooms of the Winter Palace were reconstructed. For example, a large exhibition hall emerged in the 1930s on the place previously taken by the Main Palace Buffet. Nowadays it houses an exhibition of the Department of the East devoted to the culture of Ancient Egypt. The exhibition displays works created in the course of 4,000 years from the pre-dynastic period (late 5th – 4th millennium B.C.) to the Macedonian Ptolemaic Dynasty (4th to 1st century B.C.).

The most remarkable monuments of the Middle Kingdom (21st to 17th century B.C.) include the porphyry statue of Pharaoh Amenemkhet III, who ruled Egypt in the nineteenth century B.C. During his reign, in the period of flowering of the Middle Kingdom, unique irrigation structures were built. This statue is a fine example of royal sculptural portraiture. The pharaoh's calm and majestic figure is traditional, he has a *names* (a striped kerchief of the Egyptian pharaohs) decorated with an *uraeus* (the snake-shaped emblem of royal power) on his head. The head with prominent cheek-bones and the chin betraying will-power were given an individual treatment. The throne is carved with the names and titles of the sovereign of the Nile.

A true masterpiece of the New Kingdom (16th to 11th century B.C.) is a small statuette of a young man (15th century B.C.) carved of ebony wood. The body of the youth is softly modelled, there are no sharp lines and the craftsman emphasized not the warrior's physical might, as was usual for earlier works, but the effeminacy of the refined courtier. The depicted youth was evidently one of the closest associates of Amenkhotep III, sphinxes from the burial temple of whom decorated the Neva embankment in St Petersburg. The facial features of the courtier seem to be reminiscent of his ruler. Starting from the Middle Kingdom, the Egyptians began to depict themselves as looking like their ruling pharaoh.

The stele of Ipi, the pharaoh's scribe and palace manager, dates from the New Kingdom (first half of the 14th century B.C). The stele was evidently created for his tomb. Ipi is shown in a traditional genuflecting posture adoring Anubis, the god-embalmer of the dead, who was traditionally depicted as a jackal or a man with the head of this beast.

The display also includes wooden and stone sarcophagi, mummies, faience decorations, wooden figurines of servants, sculptural depictions of gods, papyri, fabrics and other memorial objects. Most of these exhibits came from tombs and were connected with a burial rite exceptionally developed in Ancient Egypt.

**Statuette of a young man.
15th century A.D. Wood**

**Culture of Ancient Egypt.
Part of the display**

**Statue of Pharoh Amenemkhet III.
19th century B.C. Porphyry.**

Stele of Ipi. 14th century B.C. Limestone

The artifacts found by archaeologists in the Pazyryk burial mounds in the Altai Mountains in 1947–49 are famous all over the world. In ancient times robbers penetrated to the Altai burials and ravished golden articles, but later the robbers' hole was filled with water that turned into ice in the burial pit for centuries, and permafrost ensured unique state of preservation of articles made of wood, leather and fabric from the fifth–fourth centuries B.C.

A huge felt carpet is executed in the colour appliqué technique. The same design recurs on the white felt: a warrior coming up to the goddess seated on the throne.

A large wooden chariot is notable for its unique state of preservation.

The earliest of felt carpets known to us was probably brought from Central Asia or Iran.

The remains of horses in the Pazyryk burial mounds became mummified in permafrost. The horse attire and other objects show scenes of beast fighting, with a recurrent motif – the struggle of a predatory beast with herbivorous animals. Such depictions, done in a highly expressive manner, became known as the "beast

style". A fine example of this style is a wooden carved object with a depiction of a griffin tearing a deer's hand.

Felt carpet. 4th century B.C.
Fifth Pazyryk burial mound
Detail

Wooden chariot.
5th–4th century B.C.
Fifth Pazyryk burial mound

Pazyryk burial mounds.
5th–4th century B.C.
Finds from horse burials

Felt carpet. 4th century B.C.
Fifth Pazyryk burial mound. Detail

Griffin. Wooden decoration
of male head-dress. 5th–4th century B.C.
Second Pazyryk burial mound

**Deer. Plaque for a shield or quiver.
7th century B.C. Gold.
Kostroma burial mound**

**Coiling panther. Plaque. 7th–6th century
B.C. Gold. Siberian Collection of Peter the Great**

**Comb. 5th–4th century B.C. Gold.
Solokha burial mound**

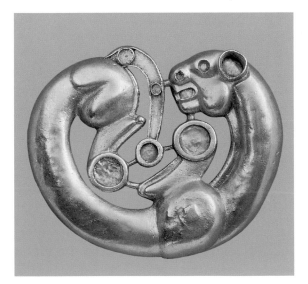

One of the two exhibitions of the Hermitage's Treasure Gallery is situated on the ground floor of the Winter Palace. Its first rooms display ancient works from precious metals and gemstones. Many objects were found in burials scattered on an immense space from the steppes of the Northern Black Sea Coast to Siberia, where nomadic tribes, whose art is referred to as the "beast style", dwelled in the first millennium B.C.

The first objects in the "beast style" were found in Siberia and it was Peter the Great himself who started to collect them. A notable example from the Emperor's Siberian collection is a fine plaque shaped like a coiling panther (7th–6th century B.C.), executed from gold – the metal regarded as sacred in olden times.

The steppes near the Northern Caucasus and the Black Sea Area were inhabited by the Scythians. A masterpiece of the Scythian "beast style" is a golden deer (7th century B.C.) discovered in the Kuban River area, in a burial mound near the village of Kostromskaya. The stylized depiction of an animal was a divine image for ancient nomads. This massive golden plaque, endowed with magic defensive power, was attached to a shield or quiver of a noble Scythian.

The famous golden comb, crowned with a sculptural group of fighting Scythians is a find from the Solokha burial mound (the Dnieper area). The comb was produced in the late fifth – early fourth century B.C. by Greek masters, who lived next to the Scythians in the towns-colonies of the Northern Black Sea Coast. The figures skillfully executed by the Greeks, give an idea about the appearance of the Scythians, their clothing and weapons. This is one of the objects testifying to close contacts between the Scythian and Greek worlds.

The Kul-Oba burial mound (4th century B.C.) was situated on the territory of the Bosporan Kingdom established by Greek colonies at the Northern Black Sea Coast, near present-day Kerch or former Panticapeum – the capital of the Bosporan Kingdom. The flat Greek bowl – phial – comes from this rich burial. Its outer surface is covered all over with a relief pattern, perfectly matching the form of this ritual vessel for libations. It was also at Kul-Oba that the famous electrum vessel was produced by Greek masters, but Scythian in shape and bearing relief representations of Scythians. The same barrow yielded golden temple pendants that used to be attached to a head-gear. The disc depicts the head of the famous statue of Athena, the ancient Greek goddess of wisdom and just war. It is likely that this is the earliest depiction of the statue of this goddess created by the great Pheidias for the Parthenon in Athens.

Ritual bowl. 4th century B.C. Gold. Kul-Oba burial mound

Vessel. 4th century B.C. Electrum. Kul-Oba burial mound

Temple pendant. 4th century B.C. Gold. Kul-Oba burial mound

The Theodosian earrings of the fourth century B.C., named after the site of their discovery (the necropolis in the town of Theodosia), were manufactured by Greek goldsmiths in the so-called microtechnique. In the nineteenth century famous jewelers of Paris and St Petersburg tried to copy them but failed.

The golden diadem from the Khokhlach burial mound near Novocherkassk (1st century A.D.), inlaid with coloured stones and glass, is an example of the "polychrome style". This luxurious object is a vivid example of the combination of ancient and barbaric cultural traditions. The diadem was created in the period when new waves of nomads (the Sarmatians and then the Alans) pushed the former tribes from the expanses of the Eurasian steppes.

The golden mask with an unusually elaborate treatment of facial features (3rd century A.D.) was discovered in Kerch, in the burial of Reskuporides III, a ruler of the Bosporan Kingdom.

Earring. 4th century B.C. Gold.
The Theodosia Necropolis

Burial mask. 3rd century B.C. Gold. Kerch

Diadem. 1st century A.D.
Gold, coloured stones and glass. Khokhlach burial mound

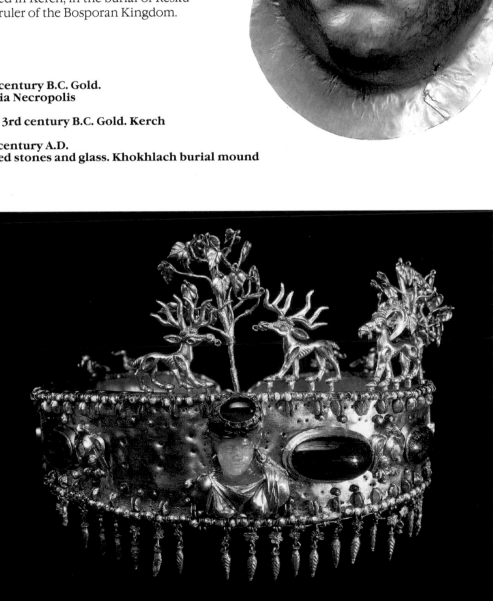

Jug. 17th century. Gold, silver, diamonds,
rubies, emeralds and pearls. India

Plate. 17th century. Gold, enamel, diamonds,
rubies and emeralds. India

Table. Made by Situram. 17th century. Gold, enamel,
diamonds, rubies, emeralds and pearls. India

Jug. 16th–17th century. Rock crystal,
gold, silver, emeralds, rubies and turquoise.
Italy, Turkey

Dagger and sheath. 17th century.
Steel, gold, wood, emeralds, rubies,
pearls and paste. India, Iran

Besides ancient articles, represented in the Goldroom are fourteenth-to nineteenth-century jewellery objects from the East. Most luxurious are seventeenth-century items from the treasury of the Great Moguls captured in Delhi by the ruler of Iran Nadir Shah and sent by him to Russia in 1739 as a diplomatic gift. The main role in their décor belongs to gemstones – the surfaces are covered all over with rubies, emeralds, diamonds and pearls. These objects include a small jar, a plate with a festooned edge and a miniature table-stand, with an inscription on the inner side calling its producer the "one strewing with gems".

The display includes superb Oriental weapons – Iranian, Indian and Turkish daggers and sabres, their blades are often made of the famous damask steel and their hilts and sheaths are decorated with precious stones.

Some pieces are assembled of parts produced in different times and in different countries. Thus, the method of fixing gems on the hilt and on the sheath mouth of one of the museum's steel daggers is characteristic of seventeenth-century Indian objects, while the sheath itself is of Iranian work of the same century. The jug, the body of which had been carved of rock crystal in sixteenth-century Italy, had lost its top and foot before coming to Turkey, where in the seventeenth century it was provided with a new foot, neck and handles and also adorned with gems.

Created in the 1850s, the Pavilion Hall occupies nearly the entire first floor of the Northern Pavilion in the Small Hermitage, hence its name. Impressive and ornate, it strikes one by the erudition and imagination of its architect. Andrei Stackenschneider, one of leading architects of the Historical style, skillfully combined here artistic traditions of different countries and ages. The light, freely standing two-tiered arcade, the gallery with elegant corner balconies and a gilded pattern of railings, the staircase "sunk" into a marble wall – all evokes associations with Moresque architecture. Oriental motif can be also revealed in the four wall fountains – variations of the "Fountain of Tears" from the palace of the Crimean Khan in Bakhchisarai, where drops of water were slowly falling from the upper marble shells to lower ones like tears. Renaissance motifs can be detected in the moulded décor. The mosaic floor of the hall is a quote from ancient art. This is a smaller replica of the mosaic that once had adorned the floor of ancient Roman thermae in the town of Ocriculum. Depicted here are some characters of ancient myths – the head of Medusa the Gorgon, centaurs and inhabitants of the sea kingdom.

The décor of the interior is supplemented with numerous crystal chandeliers.

The Pavilion Hall.
Architect: Andrei Stackenschneider. 1850–58

The Pavilion Hall. North-western section

One of the most famous exhibits of the Pavilion hall is the Peacock Clock, produced by the well-known English clockmaker James Cox. The clock was purchased for Prince Grigory Potemkin and was intended for Catherine the Great. Brought in 1781 from England in a dismantled state, the clock could be assembled and put in working order only more than ten years later by the talented Russian craftsman Ivan Kulibin. This fine automatic piece functions since 1794.

The dial of the clock is arranged in the cap of a large mushroom that "grew up" under an oak. A special mechanism sets the figures of birds in motion. The owl is the first to "get alive", it turns its head and blinks its eyes, its cage rotates and the bells ring. Then the peacock graciously bends its head, spreads its luxurious tale and turns slowly. The cockerel is the last to start its movement and singing.

James Cox. The *Peacock* Clock.
Second half of the 18th century

**The Romanov Gallery with
the display of medieval European art**

**Reliquary bearing a representation
of a legend about St Valeria
Limoges. 1175–80**

**Rogier van der Weyden
St Luke Painting the Virgin
16th century**

In the nineteenth century the western gallery of the Small Hermitage housed portraits of the Romanov dynasty, hence its name – the Romanov Gallery. Today the other section of the gallery is given to the display of Western European applied art of the Middle Ages. Represented here are church plate and secular objects executed in a variety of materials: carved wooden furniture, bronze vessels for water, copper caskets-reliquaries embellished with enamels, decorative ceramic ware, small folding altarpieces, ivory statuettes of the Virgin, etc. Worthy of special attention among ceramic articles is a large fifteenth-century vase that once had adorned Alhambra, the palace of the Moorish rulers in Granada (Spain). Purchased in the nineteenth century by the Spanish artist Fortuny, it got his name. A masterpiece of the collection is the so-called casket of St Valeria (12th century). The copper reliquary-casket in the form of a Roman cathedral is embellished with scenes from the life of St Valeria, a Roman martyr, who was executed for her secret adoption of Christianity, but then herself brought her cut-off head to the Christian bishop. The representations are executed in the technique of champlevé enamel, for which the craftsmen of the French town of Limoges were famous.

In the southern part of the Romanov Gallery one can see the collection of Netherlandish art of the fifteenth and sixteenth centuries. The picture *St Luke Painting the Virgin* gives a fairly good notion of the creative manner of Rogier van der Weyden (*ca* 1400–1464), one of major artists of the fifteenth century. It is based on a legend that the Evangelist Luke painted the Virgin when she appeared to him. The Apostle was thought to be the first icon-painter and the patron of artists – their guild in Europe was named after him.

A painter of the Netherlandish Renaissance, Van der Weyden represents the characters of the Holy Scripture in a familiar world and in the spirit of his age giving a detailed description of it. The figurines in the second plane are the parents of the Virgin Mary, Joachim and Anne, who contemplate the panoramic view of a fifteenth-century city. The generalized image of Mary apparently personified the artist's notion about the ideal female type, while the face of St Luke is endowed with individual features reminding us that Rogier was an outstanding portrait painter. Behind the half-opened door of the cell one can see a bull – the attribute of the Evangelist St Luke.

The triptych by Hugo van der Goes (*ca* 1440 – 1482) was based on subjects from Christ's life. The central composition of the three-partite altarpiece depicts *The Adoration of the Magi,* the scene on the left-hand wing shows *The Circumcision* and the right-hand one, *The Massacre of the Innocents.* The vivid emotionality of the images, the dramatic atmosphere, the tension of the colour range, characteristic of the artistic idiom of the triptych, are distinctive features of this master, one of the most remarkable artists of his time.

Landscape with a Scene from the Legend of St Christopher by Jan Mandyn (active in the early sixteenth century) is filled with fantastic images inspired by the work of the famous Hieronymus Bosch, whose follower Mandyn was. The scene with St Christopher is placed in the foreground of the picture, at the left. Legend has it that the saint, whose name means "Christ-bearer", carried the Infant Jesus over a torrent.

The Adoration of the Magi by Pieter Brueghel the Younger (*ca* 1564–1638) is a copy executed by the artist from a work by his father, the great sixteenth-century master Pieter Brueghel the Elder, whose paintings (like paintings by Bosch) are not represented in the Hermitage.

**Pieter Brueghel the Younger. *The Adoration of the Magi*
Second half of the 16th century (?)**

**Jan Mandyn. *Landscape with the Scene of a Legend
about St Christopher.* Early 16th century**

Hugo van der Goes. *The Adoration of the Magi.* Triptych. 15th century

them with a spiritual quality. A masterpiece of the collection is *The Madonna* from the *Annunciation* Scene by Simone Martini (*ca* 1284–1344). The major Sienese master of the fourteenth century won renown thanks to the special poetic quality of his images and his refined manner, which is characterized by a resilient linear design and exquisite decorativeness. The Madonna is listening to the Archangel Gabriel who announced to her, according to the Gospel of St Luke, about the forthcoming birth of the Son of God through her. She is a personification of fragile femininity, elegance and lyricism. The composition was conceived as the right wing of a diptych presenting the appearance of the heavenly messenger to St Mary. The left wing with the figure of the Archangel can be found in the National Gallery in Washington.

The Madonna and Child with Angels, a work by the outstanding Florentine artist Fra Beato Angelico (1395–1455), dates from the next century. The features of medieval artistic language – the frame in the form of a Gothic arch, the golden background – are combined here with such novel artistic means as the light and shade modelling of forms.

The first floor of the Old (Large) Hermitage, put up between 1771 and 1787 to a project by Yury Velten, houses the displays of Italian art of the thirteenth to sixteenth century. In the first hall one can see works created in the thirteenth and fourteenth centuries and commonly known as "primitives". Produced in the period of transition from the Middle Ages to the Renaissance, they are marked by Late Gothic features and elements of Byzantine icon-painting. The gilded background symbolize divine light and designate heavenly space, and the elongated proportions of fleshless figures serve to endow

Simone Martini.
The *Madonna* from the *Annunciation* Scene. 1340–44

Fra Beato Angelico. *The Madonna and Child with Four Angels. Ca* 1425

The Hall of Italian Primitives.
Architect: Andrei Stackenschneider. 1851–58

Many of the works represented in the first hall of Italian art were originally sections of many-partite altarpieces. Thus, the works of the fourteenth-century painter Spinello Aretino, *St Pontian* and *St Benedict*, which have retained their Gothic frames, had one served as wings of a polyptych. The interiors of the Old Hermitage, originally intended for the arrangement of art collections, were later used as palatial apartments. In 1851–60 Andrei Stackenschneider, an architect of the Historical style, redecorated them lavishly employing for their décor various kinds of wood, coloured stones, gilding, moulding and painting. Especially impressive is the décor of the largest hall of the Neva Enfilade treated in the spirit of the Grand Style that took shape in French art of the seventeenth century. Now this interior is known as the Leonardo da Vinci Room.

The Leonardo da Vinci Room. Architect: Andrei Stackenschneider. 1859

Leonardo da Vinci. *The Madonna and Child (The Benois Madonna)*. 1478

One can see in this room the two paintings by Leonardo da Vinci (1452–1519) owned by the Hermitage. *The Benois Madonna,* previously kept in the family of the architect Leonty Benois (hence its name) and acquired for the museum in 1914, illustrates the early period in the work of the great Florentine master of the Renaissance. In keeping with the tradition of the fifteenth century – the period known as the Early Renaissance – the holy subject is interpreted as a natural, lively genre scene. The image of the young Mary, with her clothing and hairstyle corresponding to the fashion of Leonardo da Vinci's time, personifies the joy of motherhood. The flower with four petals, handed over by the Madonna to Jesus, symbolizes the cross and reminds us about the future Crucifixion. At the same time the gesture of the Child's hand persistently stretching towards the plant, implies man's striving to cognize the world, which was so typical of Leonardo himself as a scholar and artist. Numerous anatomical studies of the young master helped him convincingly convey the poses and gestures of the characters, the specific features of the childish body and to clearly define the proportions of the figures. The picture is executed in oils, then a new medium for Italy, and Leonardo used its possibilities for developing subtle light-and-shade gradations.

The Litta Madonna, acquired for the Hermitage in 1865 from Count Litta, dates from the period when Leonardo da Vinci was active in Milan at the court of Duke Lodovico Moro. The elevated atmosphere of the painting filled with harmony is characteristic of the High Renaissance. The barely visible smile in the corners of Mary's lips not only does not break the classical features of the Madonna's face, but lends a special charm to the ideally beautiful image. The painter employed traditional symbolism: the Madonna's red dress and blue cloak are the clothes of the Heavenly Queen, the red-headed bird in the hand of Jesus is the sign of blood to be shed by Him.

Portrait of a Woman by Correggio (1489–1534), a major representative of the Parma school, confirms the fact that Leonardo's influence was truly great – the sitter's posture (probably this is the poet Ginevra Rangone) suggests a resemblance to the pose of Gioconda in Leonardo's famous painting now in the Louvre in Paris. This likeness is Correggio's rare work in this genre.

The authorship of *Flora* that had earlier been considered the work of Leonardo da Vinci is now ascribed to his favourite pupil, Francesco Melzi (1493 – *ca* 1570). The ancient goddess of spring and flowers holds an aquilegia (columbine) in her hand – a flower that gave the picture its former name, *Columbine.*

Correggio. *Portrait of a Woman. Ca* 1519

Francesco Melzi. *Flora.* 1510–15

Leonardo da Vinci
The Madonna and Child (The Litta Madonna). 1490s

The halls of the suite located over the courtyard of the Old Hermitage are devoted to the art of Venice – a powerful republic, the "Queen of Seas" and the "pearl of the Adriatic Sea", thought to be patronized by St Marc. Venetian painting had retained the traditions of Byzantine culture right until the middle of the fifteenth century, when art of the Early Renaissance began to develop not only in Florence, where Renaissance culture inspired by a turn to Classical Antiquity began to emerge, but all over Italy. Nevertheless trodding the path of Renaissance art, painters of the republic of St Marc not only mastered the new artistic idiom just within several decades, but created a powerful art school famous for its vivid, life-asserting spirit as well as for the wealth and expressiveness of its colour solutions.

The establishment of the High Renaissance in the Venetian Republic was associated with the work of Giorgione (1478?–1510), an artist belonging to the galaxy of great European masters. His *Judith,* based on a subject of an apocryphal Old Testament legend about the deed of a widow from Bethulia, a town in Judaea, became a symbol of the picture gallery of the Hermitage.

On coming to the camp of the Assyrian army that had besieged Bethulia, Judith seduced the army commander Holofernes by her beauty and then, after a feast held in her honour, cut off the head of the enemy's commander by his sword and thus saved her people from the conquerors. The image of the heroine, trampling the head of the defeated enemy, with a strange smile arrested on his face, personifies both the magnificence of the heroic feat and the charm of femininity. The calm, permeating Judith's pure soul, corresponds to an idyllic quietness of the poetic scenery.

In 1968–71 Hermitage restorers uncovered Giorgione's painting from later overpaintings and darkened varnish and this measure made visible some previously hidden details of the painting and its subtle colour nuances.

The work of Titian (*ca* 1488–1576), the head of the brilliant Venetian school that mastered and continued the traditions of Giorgione, is represented in the museum by paintings in a variety of genres and from different periods. His *Danaë,* belonging to the period of the great artist's creative maturity, is one of several versions of the same Greek myth produced by Titian. The artist, inspired by Greek and Roman mythology throughout her life, referred to such pictures devoted to ancient subjects, extremely popular in the age of the Renaissance, as *poesie.*

Akrisias, the King of Argos, whom the oracle foretold to die from the hand of his future grandson, decided to hide his only daughter Danaë in a secret tower where only an old woman served her. The King, however, failed to evade the predestination – Zeus himself, delighted with the beauty of the young captive, appeared to her in the form of golden rain, treated by the painter as a stream of golden coins. Depicting the moment of Danaë's miraculous meeting with her divine lover, Titian created a poetic hymn to life and love. Danaë is an embodiment of the beauty of female body according to the notion of the celebrated Venetian – she is both sensual and chaste, earthly and perfect. A great role in the creation of an optimistic, life-asserting atmosphere of the painting belongs to its warm colour scheme, rich in nuances and permeated with light.

Titian. *Danaë. Ca* **1554**

Giorgione. *Judith.* **Before 1504**

The pride of the Hermitage collection is a group of Titian's later paintings that he had kept at home until his death. These include *Repentant Mary Magdalene,* a masterpiece that won renown even during the life of its creator. The subject of the picture is taken from a Christian legend about a sinner who became Christ's follower and retreated to a desert so as to devote herself to repentance and prayer. Near the hermit one can see her attribute – a vessel with a holy oil; in front of her is a prayer book lying on a skull – a traditional symbol of the transitory character of all earthly things.

The painter created an image of a passionate and strong personality that had underwent a deep moral change. Magdalene's lofty spirit is in harmony with her perfect body. Titian implemented in his protagonist the Venetian ideal of full-blooded, sensual beauty. At the same time the picture conveys with a breath-taking vivacity the suffering of the troubled soul echoed by nature that is full of tension and anxiety. The dramatic atmosphere is created by the colour range, in which chromatic contrasts combine with a subtle treatment of shades and reflexes, the disquiet lighting and the energetic draughtsmanship, striking us by a variety of the employed means.

The world-famous *St Sebastian* was one of the great Venetian's last works. He depicted the execution of the Roman warrior who secretly adopted Christianity, as legend has it, and Emperor Diocletian ordered to shoot him from bows. The image of the saint reflects a notion about an ideally beautiful hero formed in the age of the Renaissance. It is not accidental that the youth's figure and posture are reminiscent of the famous ancient statue of Apollo Belvedere – creating the image of an ideal man. Renaissance artists followed the traditions of ancient art drawing inspiration from the classical proportions and noble plasticity of ancient art.

Titian. *St Sebastian. Ca* **1570**

Titian. *Repentant Mary Magdalene.* **1560s**

The arrows pierced St Sebastian's nude torso, flames of fire are near his feet, but the martyr's courage and spiritual might contrast with his physical sufferings. The surrounding world interpreted as a gloomy chaos, seems to echo the man's drama. Only some details – a bush growing near the pole to which the saint is tied and scarlet reflexes in the sky – are barely discerned in the landscape.

The deeply tragic atmosphere of the picture is largely created by its chromatic solution reminding us that colour is the essential component of the Venetian artistic idiom. The intensity of the colour scheme developed down to minute nuances, is enhanced by outbursts of separate colour spots. The brushstrokes characteristic of Titian's dynamic, temperamental manner form a vibrant, moving, agitated texture.

The Raphael Loggias form a gallery that repeats, with some alterations, the famous Loggias of the Vatican Palace, the construction of which was started by the architect Donato Bramante and completed by the great painter and architect Raphael (1483–1520). The master's pupils carried out the painting of the loggias from his drawings under his supervision and completed the decoration in 1519.

The Hermitage's Loggias, created at the behest of Catherine the Great, were put up to a project by Giacomo Quarenghi and a group of artists led by Christoph Unterberger (1732–1798) made copies of frescoes on canvas in Rome for them. Arranged on the vaults of the gallery are 25 compositions – the cycle called the "Raphael Bible". The ensemble that implemented a synthesis of arts characteristic of the Renaissance was completed in 1792. Later the gallery was incorporated into the complex of halls of the New Hermitage.

The Raphael Loggias in the Hermitage. Detail of painting

The Raphael Loggias in the Hermitage. 1780s. Architect: Giacomo Quarenghi

The Conestabile Madonna named after its former owner is one of Raphael's best works. The celebrated artist began his career in painting with small-scale works characteristic of the Early Renaissance. A tribute to this tradition is his meticulous treatment of details. The panoramic landscape in the composition is inspired by the poetic scenery of Umbria, the artist's homeland. The picture in the form of *tondo* (a circle in Italian) has retained its original frame produced evidently from a drawing by Raphael himself.

Raphael. *The Madonna and Child (The Conestabile Madonna).* 1504

The Raphael Room (Hall of Italian Majolica) in the New Hermitage. Architect: Leo von Klenze . 1850–52

The Raphael Room, decorated in the spirit of Renaissance art and displaying, in addition to Raphael's works, Italian majolicas of the fifteenth and sixteenth centuries, is a fine interior on the first floor of the New Hermitage. The halls and rooms of this building, designed specially for the preservation of art collections, preserved not only their original décor, but in many cases their natural connection with the exhibitions displayed in them.

Mounted in the walls of one of the Cabinets – little rooms intended mainly for small-scale works – are frescoes of the Raphael school. Executed by pupils of the great artist in 1523–24, they originally adorned the loggia at a villa on Palatine Hill in Rome. The general theme of the cycle is the story of Venus, the ancient goddess of love and beauty.

The Crouching Boy by Michelangelo (1475–1564), also displayed here, is the only work of the great master in Russian museums. Catherine the Great acquired it in 1785. The sculpture owes its traditional name to the posture of the young athlete. The chisel of the great sculptor seems to let the compact, monolithic statue out of a square marble block merely by removing unnecessary pieces of stone. The unfinished shapes, the barely suggested details and roughness of the unpolished marble do not diminish this impression.

The physical might of the youth conveys a heroic quality, but at the same time his body is bent and bound by his depressed spirit. A contrast between the force of strained muscles and a profound inner suffering creates a dramatic tension that is typical of those images by Michelangelo, which reflected the crisis of the Renaissance world outlook.

Some scholars assume that Michelangelo created *The Crouching Boy* for the sculptural décor of the Medici Chapel in the San Lorenzo Church in Florence.

Several Cabinets display works by Italian masters of the seventeenth century, a period that was called the Golden Age of European painting.

The Lute Player is the only canvas in Russia by Carravaggio (1571–1610), a great artist who made a revolution in painting by turning to earthly reality. The painter's careful attention to the real world is revealed in the way he rendered the palpable material quality of

the youth's figure and the still-life objects with all their distinctive features. Caravaggio most important innovatory device is the emphasis on powerful light and shade contrasts.

In front of the lute player is an opened sheet of music of the madrigal "You know that I love you" by the sixteenth-century composer Jacob Arcadelt. The work that seems to be a usual everyday scene at first glance is an allegory of love, with symbols of the five senses and the transitive character of earthly life (the worn-out sheet of music and the broken strings of the violin).

Michelangelo Merisi da Caravaggio
The Lute Player. Ca 1595

The Hall of Frescoes of the School of Raphael
Architect: Leo von Klenze . 1851

Michelangelo. *The Crouching Boy.* **1530–34**

The Suite of Cabinets runs parallel to the larger top-lit interiors – the three halls with glazed ceilings, hence the names of skylight halls given to them. The vast unbroken surfaces of the walls of the top-lit rooms were intended for large-scale paintings. In the Small Skylight Hall, among works by Italian masters of the sixteenth and seventeenth centuries, is the monumental canvas *Birth of St John the Baptist* by Tintoretto (1518–1594), one of the most prominent Venetian painters active in the second half of the sixteenth century. The Gospel event is represented in a contemporary interior dominated by agitation natural for the occasion: the servants are bustling about, the wet-nurse is bowing over the newly born child lying in the Virgin's arms (according to the Gospels, Elisabeth, John's mother, was a relation of the Virgin Mary). In the depth of the painting is a bed with the woman in childbirth, on the right is Zachariah, the child's father, who had not believed to the Angel announcing to him about the birth of a son and for that God punished him with muteness. He regained the gift of speaking only when the child had been born. The treatment of the subject in the spirit of a genre scene is combined with a heightened mood created by the intense colour combinations and expressive treatment – the devices typical of Tintoretto's artistic manner.

The painting *The Death of Cleopatra* by the Neapolitan master Massimo Stanzione (1585–1656) treats a theme from ancient history popular in the seventeenth century. The Queen of Egypt, on becoming a prisoner of Emperor Octavian, died from a bite of a snake brought on her order.

Tintoretto. *Birth of St John the Baptist.* 1550s

Massimo Stanzione. *The Death of Cleopatra.* 1630s–1640s

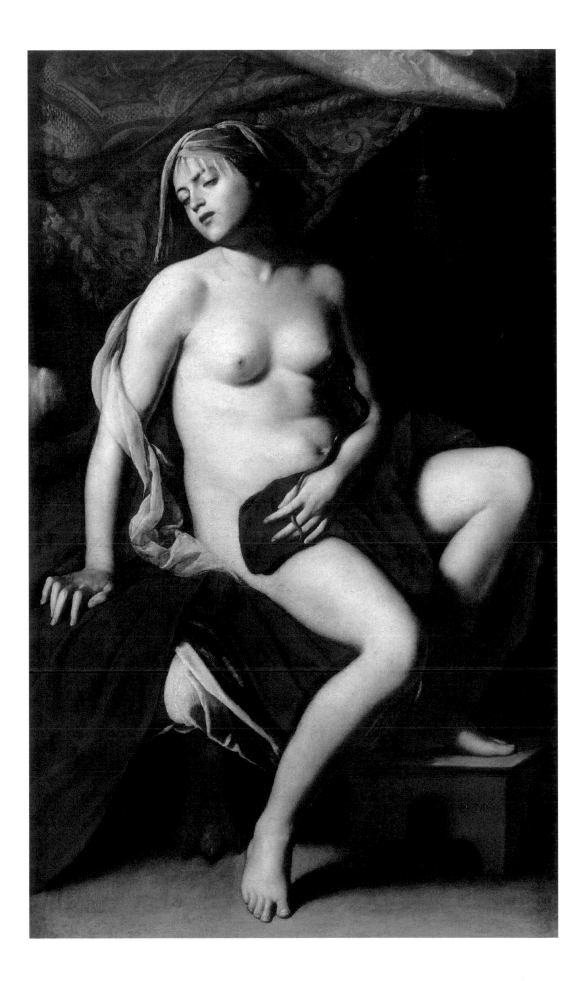

The effective décor of the Large Skylight Hall – the central and largest of the three skylight interiors – reminds us that the New Hermitage was conceived as an addition integrated with the luxurious imperial residence. The original décor of the hall included the article of coloured stones made by Russian craftsmen in the nineteenth century.

Among the exhibited works of the Italian masters of the seventeenth and eighteenth centuries stand out the monumental canvases of the Venetian Giovanni Battista Tiepolo (1696–1770), the last great artist of the Baroque style. Five of them belong to the series of pictures treating heroic subjects from ancient Roman history and glorifying in a symbolic form the Venetian Republic equal to Rome in its grandeur. The largest canvas, *Triumph of the Army Commander Manius Curius Dandatus,* depicts a return of the army that defeated the army of Pyrrhus, King of Epirus, and captured prisoners and elephants.

The famous master of the *vedute* (cityscape) Antonio Canal, called Canaletto (1697– 1868), depicted in his painting *Reception of the French Ambassador in Venice* a real episode and convincingly depicted the majestic appearance of the city vividly unfolding all the magnificence of its architecture and the unusual character of its daily life.

◄ **The Large Italian Skylight Hall.**
Architect: Leo von Klenze . 1851

Antonio Canal
***Reception of the French Ambassador in Venice.* 1726–27**

Giovanni Battista Tiepolo
***Triumph of the Army Commander Manius Curius Dandatus.* 1728–30**

Represented in the Spanish Skylight Hall and the nearby Cabinet is Spanish art of the fifteenth to the seventeenth century. The Hermitage collection of Spanish painting, one of the most remarkable outside Spain, abounds in pictures by major masters.

A gem of the collection is the painting *The Apostles Peter and Paul* by the great El Greco (1541–1614), as Domenikos Theotokopoulos, an artist of Greek descent active in Toledo, was called. The principal Apostles of the Church are shown discussing the church doctrine. The argument reveals the opposite characters of the saints – the meek Peter holding a key from the gates of Paradise in his hands and the strong-willed Paul, a convinced advocate of Christianity, resting on a book. The specific features of El Greco's pictorial manner can be easily recognized in his temperamental, dynamic brushstrokes, in the elongated proportions of the body and in colour contrasts. The master's artistic devices serve to create a powerful emotional expressiveness inherent to his works.

The Virgin with a Distaff is a fine example of the later work of Luis Morales (*ca* 1509 – 1586), an artist from the Spanish province of Estremadura. Inspired by mystical beliefs, the artist created unusually vivid and emotionally saturated images tinged with tragic spirit and religious exaltation. His smooth, enamel-like painting is characterized by an agitated tension of its colour scheme, in which cold, dark tones prevail, and by the sharpness of drawing recalling the expressive lines of medieval art. At the same time, having familiarized himself with works by Italian masters of the Renaissance, the Spanish painter adapted the artistic devices developed by the Italians. The subject of *The Madonna with a Distaff* was probably inspired to him by Leonardo's paintings, moreover that the depictions of the Madonna and Child, widespread in Italy, were not characteristic of Spanish art in the sixteenth century. The soft modelling used to render the volumes in Morales's painting, suggests the influence of Leonardo's famous light and shade effect – *sfumato*. The clear-cut, stable composition also reveals a similarity to the structural principles of Italian paintings. The distaff in the form of cross in the hands of Jesus is a symbol of the future passion of the Son of God and his crucifixion on the hill of Golgotha.

One of outstanding works in the collection of seventeenth-century Spanish painting is *The Girlhood of the Virgin* by Francisco de Zurbarán (1598–1664),

an original artist, who naturally combined the artistic idiom of his time with national traditions. The theme of his intimate canvas executed by Zurbarán at the end of his life passed throughout the creative career of the celebrated master. The image of praying Mary as a girl charms us by its spirituality and depth of feeling. It is supposed that the touching yet serious child's face conveys the features of the painter's daughter. Although this painting is small in size and has a concise composition, it still betrays a monumental quality characteristic of Surbarán's works.

El Greco.
The Apostles Peter and Paul.
Between 1587 and 1592

Luis de Morales.
*The Madonna and Child
with a Cross-Shaped Distaff.* 1570s

Francisco de Zurbarán.
The Girlhood of the Virgin. Ca 1660

Rembrandt Harmensz van Rijn. *Flora*. 1634

Rembrandt Harmensz van Rijn. *Danaë*. 1636

One of several rooms in the New Hermitage, where the display of Dutch art of the seventeenth century is arranged, is devoted to paintings by Rembrandt (1606–1669). The world-famous collection of the great Dutch master, whose work became one of the peak accomplishments of the European Golden Century, consists of works of different genres and different periods – from the artist's early canvases to those produced at the end of his life.

One of the young Rembrandt's masterpieces is *Flora,* representing the ancient Roman goddess of spring and flowers. Her attributes are a lavish wreath and a shaft woven with plants. Her luxurious costume, created by the artist's imagination, was probably inspired by theatrical productions. The painting was executed in the year when Rembrandt married Saskia van Uylenburgh. The appearance of the goddess, whose face betrays some resemblance to that of the master's young wife, is far from classical standards. It probably implements the ideal of beauty Rembrandt had under the impression of unassuming charm and specific femininity of Dutch women.

The famous *Danaë* is devoted to the same subject taken from ancient mythology as Titian's painting produced a century before. Like the Venetian master, Rembrandt depicted a moment when Zeus penetrates to the king's daughter hidden from people. The magic golden light, in which the god, who fell in love with Danaë, appears to her, floods all around her. An old servant is peeping from behind the curtain of a luxurious bed.

In 1985 *Danaë* suffered from an act of vandalism. For twelve years Hermitage restorers worked with the painting poured with hydrochloric acid, and in 1997 it has appeared before visitors to the museum again.

One of the most famous masterpieces from the late period of Rembrandt's work is *The Return of the Prodigal Son*. The subject, popular with seventeenth-century artists, was taken from the Gospel parable about a youth who wasted the portion of goods received from his father as his heritage in a far country, suffered from hunger and poverty and in repentance returned to his native home. Rembrandt depicted the meeting of the unhappy wanderer with his father, who "saw him and had a compassion and ran, and fell on his neck, and kissed him." In the foreground of the monumental canvas are the figures of the main characters taken out of a semidarkness by a stream of golden light. The father's face is especially illuminated and it seems itself to emanate the light of wisdom and the nobility of his soul. The gesture of his elderly hands tenderly touching his kneeling son is a sign of forgiving and blessing. The neighbours and members of the family share the feelings of the old man and the youth.

The exact date of the execution of the picture is not known. Probably this great work was painted at the very end of Rembrandt's life to implement, as it were, all the facets of his unique creative gift.

The Rembrandt Room in the New Hermitage

Rembrandt Harmensz van Rijn
***The Return of the Prodigal Son. Ca* 1668**

The Tent-Roofed Hall of the New Hermitage owes its name to the unusual ceiling with two sloping surfaces shaped like a tent. The rafters of the ceiling adorned with rectangular recessions or caissons and with painting create an unusual decorative effect. The hall has completely retained its original architectural design and décor. Nowadays it is used to keep the stone vases of Russian work, which embellished the same interior back in the nineteenth century.

The walls of the hall and the boards for hanging pictures installed here from the very beginning are hung with paintings by seventeenth-century Dutch artists, who produced small-scale works and were thus named the "Small Dutch Masters". Such small, intimate pictures were intended for little rooms of Dutch homes.

The display presents all genres of Dutch painting of that period. Portraiture was then one of the most popular kinds of painting and therefore it attracted many well-known masters. One of the most famous portraitists of the period was Frans Hals (1581/85–1666), a painter, who created captivating, full-blooded images of his contemporaries "in a breath", in a free and daring manner.

In the seventeenth century easel painting attained a brilliant flowering both in European art as a whole and in Dutch art in particular. One of the most popular among independent kinds of painting, which took shape in this period, was the genre scene. The Hermitage picture *The Glass of Lemonade* by the outstanding Dutch master Gerard Ter Borch (1617–1681) ranks with the best genre paintings. The chosen subject – a gentleman offering a drink to a girl that suddenly got sick – is not as simple as it seems to be at first sight. By a gesture of the old lady, who by chance, as it were, opens slightly the young woman's shoulder, the artist hints that the respectable matron is a procuress, although the simple-hearted admirer does not suspect about that.

Hints and reservations alluding to the hidden message of the event portrayed were characteristic of the manner of Dutch painters as was a kind smile in the painter's attitude to his characters. Thus a somewhat crude yet life-asserting humour pervades the painting *The Revellers* created by the well-known genre painter Jan Steen (1625/26–1679), who portrayed himself and his wife in this scene. Similar to this work is *Breakfast of a Young Man* by Pieter Cornelisz van Slingeland (1640–1691), where the painter treats his protagonist with a merry irony.

The Sense of Hearing by Adriaen van Ostade (1610–1685), a master of scenes featuring common people, portrays vagabonds enthusiastically making music and is nothing but a traditional allegory from the series devoted to the five senses.

Among small, nearly miniature-like works, for which a special showcase has been arranged, one can see paintings by Gerard Dou (1613–1675), the most outstanding of the young Rembrandt's pupils and the head of the movement of the "masters of subtle painting". *Old Woman Reading* is a fine example of his filigree painting.

The ability of the Small Dutch Masters to appreciate life in its everyday manifestations and to enjoy the beauty of earthly reality was revealed in the choice of prosaic motifs and in the careful rendering of the world of material things, from the velvet of a female dress to simple kitchen utensils.

The Tent-Roofed Hall.
Architect: Leo von Klenze . 1851

Frans Hals. *Portrait of a Young Man Holding a Glove. Ca* 1650

Gerard Ter Borch
***The Glass of Lemonade. Ca* 1660**

Jan Steen. *The Revellers. Ca* 1660

Gerard Dou
Old Woman Reading. Ca 1660–65

Pieter Cornelisz van Slingeland . *Breakfast of a Young Man.* Second half of the 17th century

The display of seventeenth-century Dutch painting. Detail

Adriaen van Ostade. *Sense of Hearing* (from the *Five Senses* series). 1635

Several halls of the New Hermitage are devoted to Flemish painting of the seventeenth century. The interiors preserving their original décor are embellished, as before, with articles of coloured stones produced by Russian craftsmen. One can see here paintings of different genres that developed in this brilliant period of Flemish art. A series of large decorative canvases, *Hunts,* exemplifies the work of Paul de Voos (*ca* 1596–1678), one of the most significant animal painters. The greatest master of the still life, Frans Snyders (1579–1657) was the creator of large-scale *Shops* striking us by the abundance and variety of gifts of inexhaustibly generous nature. The seemingly careless arrangement dominating his compositions creates the feeling of fullness and dynamism of life characteristic of the Flemish Baroque.

The turbulent and merry genre scene *The Bean King* by Jacob Jordans (1593–1678), who was regarded as the leading Flemish painter after the death of the great Rubens, is one of his best paintings devoted to the theme of the popular festival of the "Three Magi" (or the "Three Kings"). The "bean king", awarded with a paper crown, is a guest who was lucky to find a bean baked in his piece of festive cake. He lifts his goblet and all those present traditionally exclaim: "The king is drinking".

The Snyders Room. Architect: Leo von Klenze . 1851

Frans Snyders. *Fruit Shop.* Between 1618 and 1621

Jacob Jordaens. *The Bean King. Ca* 1638

135

Self-Portrait by Anthonis van Dyck (1599–1641), skillfully painted in a pearl-grey tonality and marked by the elegant artistry of the imagery, is one of the best portraits painted by the famous master.

Works by Pieter Paul Rubens (1577–1640), the head of the Flemish school of painting, introduce us to different facets of the work of "the king of painters and the painter of kings". Classical Antiquity served as one of the artist's thematic sources. The subject of the painting *Roman Charity* is taken from Roman literature. The young Pero saved her father Cimon, sentenced to death of hunger, by feeding him with milk from her breast. *The Union of Earth and Water* is an allegory, in which ancient gods personify the elements: Neptune stands for water and Cybele implies the land.

Anthonis van Dyck
Self-Portrait. **Late 1620s – early 1630s**

Pieter Paul Rubens
Roman Charity (Cimon and Pero). *Ca* 1612

Pieter Paul Rubens
The Union of Earth and Water. Ca 1618

137

The Union of the Earth and Water personifies the powerful energy of life born by the symbolic union of the elements. The elevated, optimistic mood is natural for the work of the Baroque style, the artistic idiom of which is meant to express heightened emotional state and sometimes even the utmost agitation of feelings.

Rubens's masterpiece, *Perseus and Andromeda,* based on the subject from Ovid's *Metamorphoses,* is also majestic like a jubilant hymn. The ancient hero Perseus killed a sea monster and thus saved from death Andromeda, the Ethiopian King's daughter who was to be sacrificed. The heroic pathos of the work glorifying the warrior's feat and the triumph of love is created by the turbulent dynamism characteristic of the Baroque, by the complex composition crowded with figures and by the colours, iridescent with nuances and penetrated by light.

Profound feeling and tragic mood determine the emotional key of the monumental painting *The Descent from the Cross.* The Hermitage canvas is a replica of the central composition of the three-partite altarpiece created by Rubens for the Antwerp Cathedral and preserved there to this day. Christ with a beautiful, inspired face is not only an immolated victim, but also a hero whose death is an act of especial grandeur.

Pieter Paul Rubens. *Descent from the Cross. Ca* 1617–18

Pieter Paul Rubens. *Perseus and Andromeda. Ca* 1622

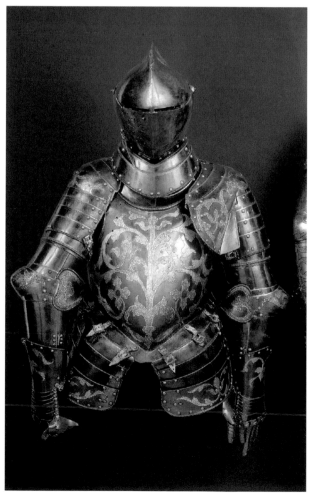

The Knights' Hall in the New Hermitage, where Western European arms and armour of the fifteenth to seventeenth century are displayed, enjoys a great interest among visitors to the museum. The exhibits from the Hermitage's Arsenal, one of the best in the world, acquaint them with offensive and defensive weapons created in the countries, which were world leaders in the field of arms an armour. The focal centre of the exhibition is the impressive equestrian group, that allows one to see, in addition to knights' armour, sixteenth-century armour for horses. One can also see here a whole set of parade armour for a horseman and his horse executed in the same style in sixteenth-century Germany. No less interesting is a corrugated "Maximilian's" armour of sixteenth-century German work (the design of this armour is ascribed to the German Emperor Maximilian I).

Arms-making was a kind of applied art – artistic metalwork that combined the efforts of armourers and artists. Their fantasy sometimes yielded original forms of articles or elaborate decorative motifs. They often borrowed ornaments and scenes depicted on arms and armour from engravings by European masters. The forms and décor of the displayed pieces correspond to the styles of art prevailing in those ages and national schools to which they belong. Thus, a helmet made in the workshop of the famous Italian smith Negroli for the jester of the Duke of Urbino was conceived as a parody on the helmet of the ruler himself made in the same Milanese workshop.

Expensive parade armour was usually made as individual commissions. As a rule the armour was commissioned for its owner's coming of age – a youth was to be knighted at twenty-one.

Craftsmen employed various techniques of metalwork for the decoration of parade armour. The half-suit amour for a pedestrian tournament produced in Germany, in the workshop of the celebrated Augsburg smith Anton Peffenhauser, is ornamented with the use of etching, engraving, metal incision and gilding. The gilded pattern blends impressively with the dark violet burnished background.

The *rondache* shield made by skilful Venetian armourers of the sixteenth century is adorned with a fine chased relief and plant ornaments executed in the technique of inlay with gold. The shield, a part of the parade set of arms and armour created for Sforza Pallavicino, the Commander-in-Chief of the Venetian Republic, bears the owner's emblem – a seven-headed hydra.

Bourguignotte helmet.
Workshop of Philippo Negroli. 1530–40

Anton Peffenhauser. Half-suit armour. 1590s

Mounted group in the Knights' Hall

Rondache shield (part of the armour
of Sforza Pallavicino). 1560–85

The Gallery of the History of Ancient Painting is a unique interior – mounted in its walls are eighty paintings that feature subjects from ancient legends and works of literature dealing with artists of Classical Antiquity and their creations. Conceived as an introduction to the halls of the New Hermitage intended for European paintings, the gallery reflected nineteenth-century notions about the history of ancient painting. The compositions were produced in Munich under the supervision of Georg Hiltensperger (1806–1890) and imitated ancient encaustics – painting in wax pigments on copper plates. Among the moulded portraits of the masters of art arranged on the pendentives of the domes one can see the likeness of Leo von Klenze, the designer of the New Hermitage.

The display of the Gallery devoted to sculpture of the late eighteenth and early nineteenth centuries includes works by the famous Danish master Bertel Thorvaldsen (1770–1824) and by the Italian Antonio Canova (1757–1822), one of the most celebrated sculptors of his age.

Antonio Canova. *Hebe.* 1800–05

Antonio Canova. *Cupid and Psyche.* 1796

Gallery of the History of Ancient Painting. Architect: Leo von Klenze . 1851

From the vestibule at the original entrance to the New Hermitage to the Gallery of the History of Ancient Painting leads a majestic staircase designed in the spirit of austere classical architecture. The clear-cut rhythm of the white marble steps divided into three flights, echoes the majestic rows of monumental granite columns soaring on the landing of the first floor. The landing is adorned by tables with mosaic tops and by vases of coloured stones. Some of them are creations by outstanding architects. For example, the vase of unusual shape with impressive bronze decorations was designed by the architect Andrei Voronikhin (1759–1814).

Also here, on the upper landing, is represented Western European sculpture of the eighteenth and nineteenth centuries. This collection was intentionally formed in the Hermitage from the early nineteenth century onwards. The most significant acquisitions were made in the reign of Nicholas I. At the Emperor's behest statues were mostly bought and commissioned in Italy, where sculptors from different European countries used to work.

The Main Staircase.
Architect: Leo von Klenze. 1851
Vase produced from a drawing
by Andrei Voronikhin. 1809

The upper landing
of the Main Staircase of the New Hermitage

Lorenzo Bartolini. (1777–1850)
Meekness. **Marble**

145

The ground floor of the New Hermitage is devoted to the art of Classical Antiquity. Created specially for the collection of ancient ceramics, the Twenty-Column Hall was designed in the spirit of classical architecture: the twenty columns divide the interior into three longitudinal sections similar to naves of an ancient temple; the floor is adorned with mosaics and the design of the ceiling resembles that of ancient structures; the painted and mosaic décor includes Greek and Roman motifs. The hall has retained its original designation and is used to this day for the display of ancient ceramic ware.

The famous Cumae vase of the fourth century B.C. was created in a Greek colony on the territory of Italy, in the maritime town of Cumae. This large black-lacquer hydria – a vessel for water – began to be called the "Queen of Vases" by lovers of antiquities in the nineteenth century.

Displayed in the same hall are monuments of Etruscan culture, mainly finds from necropolises. An outstanding example of Etruscan bronze casting is the cover of a funeral urn depicting a reclining youth (4th century B.C.).

In one of the halls, amidst works of ancient Roman sculpture, one can see the outstanding work of Russian stone-carvers of the nineteenth century – a huge vase of green wavy Revniukha jasper weighing nineteen tonnes. It was produced in the Altai Mountains, at the Kolyvan Lapidary Works.

The Twenty-Column Hall
Architect: Leo von Klenze . 1851

***Reclining Youth.* Cover of a funeral urn.**
4th century B.C. Etruria

Hydria ("The Queen of Vases". 4th century B.C.
Found in the town of Cumae, South Italy

The Kolyvan Vase. 1831–43

The Jupiter Hall derives its name from the huge statue of the ancient Roman god created in the first century A.D., in the period of the highest flowering of the Roman Empire. The impressive dimensions (the statue is 3.5 metres high), emphasized decorative character and pomposity of the statue give an idea about the tastes of the period when the famous Colosseum and the Arch of Titus were built. Jupiter holds the figurine of Victoria, the goddess of victory, in his right hand and the scepter, a symbol of supreme power, in his left hand. By the feet of the god is an eagle.

The origin of the statue of Jupiter goes down to the famous Zeus created by the ancient Greek sculptor Pheidias for the Zeus Temple in Olympia. Such use of Greek examples was characteristic of Roman sculptors and frequently it is only thanks to them that we can form some notion about the works of such famous masters as Miron, Pheidias or Praxiteles that have not reached us. The Romans collected Greek sculpture and used statuary to decorate their palaces, homes and public buildings and squares. There were workshops in Rome that specialized in copying Greek masterpieces. These and the neighbouring halls also display a superb collection of Roman sculptural portraits that numbers some 120 works and allow us to trace the evolution of this genre throughout several centuries– from the first century B.C. to the fourth century A.D.

The Jupiter Hall.
Architect: Leo von Klenze. 1851

***Statue of Jupiter.* 1st century A.D. Marble**

One of the halls of the Department of Classical Antiquity is reminiscent of an inner courtyard of an ancient home open to the sky and framed with columns in its central section. Pieces of marble decorative sculpture are represented here in a setting similar to that they had in ancient times.

The next interior, the Dionysus Hall, owes its name to the large statue of the god of wine-making. Besides decorative sculpture, it displays a masterpiece of the collection – the statue of Aphrodite, the Greek goddess of love and beauty (called Venus in Roman mythology). For some time the statue decorated the Tauride Palace of Prince Grigory Potemkin and was therefore named "Venus of Tauride". Created in the second century B.C., it was modelled on the famous statue by Praxiteles created in the 4th century B.C.

The Dionysus Hall. Architect: Leo von Klenze. 1851

Statue of Aphrodite ("Venus of Tauride").
2nd century B.C. Marble

The Roman Courtyard. Architect: Leo von Klenze. 1851

**Amphora. B.C. Silver.
Chertomlyk burial mound**

**Bullock. Mid-4th millennium B.C. Gold.
Maikop burial mound**

**Reliquary in the form of a deacon.
12th century. Wood, silver, precious
and semi-precious stones. France**

**Processional (Freiburg) cross.
Late 13th century. Wood, gold, silver, enamel,
glass, precious and semi-precious stones. Upper Rhine**

One exhibition of the Treasure Gallery is situated on the ground floor of the New Hermitage. Similarly to the other section of the Treasure Gallery situated in the Winter Palace, it opens with archaeological finds.

The objects found during excavations of the Maikop burial mound in the Northern Caucasus are older than the Egyptian pyramids – they are dated to the mid-fourth millennium B.C. Among them are two little bulls cast in gold and other two in silver.

The largest Scythian barrow, the Chertomlyk burial mound in the lower reaches of the Dnieper, yielded a large silver amphora for wine, with gilded details, created for Scythians by a Greek jeweller in the fourth century B.C.

Next to archaeological artifacts are displayed works produced in the Middle Ages and the new times. A veritable masterpiece of Roman art is a French twelfth-century silver-gilt reliquary in the shape of a deacon. No less interesting is a thirteenth-century Gothic cross notable for its perfect execution and abundant Christian symbolism. It came from a monastery near the German town of Freiburg and was intended for keeping the particles of the Life-Giving Cross.

Secular jewellery amazes visitors by its luxury. The pendants produced by European jewellers of the sixteenth and seventeenth centuries were worn both by women and men. The basic element of many of them is a pearl of an irregular shape, known as Baroque pearl. It is a pearl of such kind that forms the body of a swan made in the Netherlands.

The collection has a large variety of clocks, which had not only practical use, but served as a costume decoration, too.

The fine master of jewellery Jérémie Pauzié, who came to Russia as a youth and was active in St Petersburg for many years, produced magnificent bouquets of precious and semiprecious stones in the eighteenth century.

The last but not the least works in the display are objects made by Carl Fabergé and jewellers of his company. Worthy of special note among them is miniature copy of the imperial regalia created for the World Exhibition of 1900 in Paris, an exhibition that laid the beginning of Fabergé's worldwide fame.

Pendant: *Swan*. Late 16th century
Pearls, gold, enamel, rubies and diamonds. Netherlands

Clock. 1760s. Gold, silver, diamonds and enamel. St Petersburg

The Imperial Regalia (scale model). 1900. Gold, silver, platinum, diamonds,
spinel, pearls, sapphires, velvet and rhodonite. Fabergé Company, St Petersburg

Bouquet of flowers. By Jérémie Pauzié. 1740s. Gold, silver, diamonds,
precious and semi-precious stones, glass and fabric. St Petersburg

Cornflowers with ears of oats. Early 20th century. Gold, diamonds, enamel
and rock crystal. Fabergé Company, St Petersburg

The joint action of the State Hermitage and the Hermitage Bridge Studio devoted to
the 60th Anniversary of the Lifting of the Siege of Leningrad (2004) ➤

THE GOLD DRAWING ROOM

ROTUNDA

MALACHITE ROOM

WINTER PALACE

⇗
ENTRANCE
TO THE MUSEUM

PALACE CHURCH

Text: Yelena Klimovtseva and Regina Kogan
Translation from the Russian: Valery Fateyev
Design and layout: Yekaterina Poliak
Cover design: Inna Zezegova
Photography: Sergei Bogomiako, Leonard Kheifets,
Yury Molodkovets, Yekaterina Poliak, Victor Savik,
Yevgeny Siniaver, Georgy Skachkov,
Vladimir Terebenin and Valery Zubarov
Editor: Natalia Morozova
Type-setting: Meta Leif
Colour correction: Liubov Bogdanova,
Inna Zezegova and Tatyana Chernyshenko
Techical Director: Peter Krakovsky

ISBN 978-5-9778-0003-7

PORTICO WITH ATLANTES

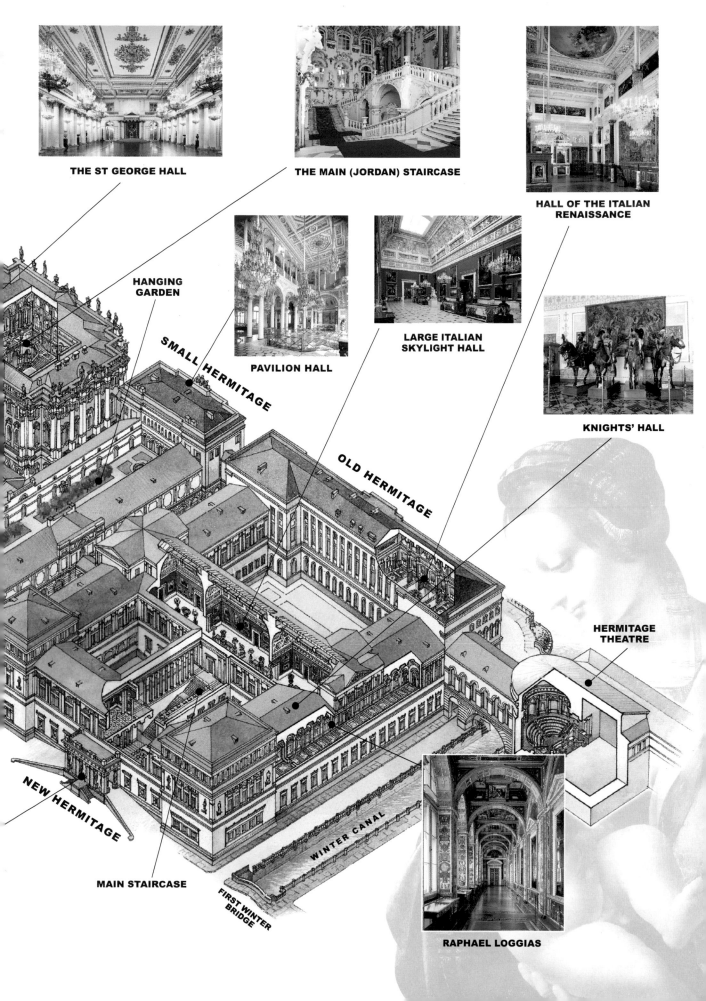

THE ST GEORGE HALL

THE MAIN (JORDAN) STAIRCASE

HALL OF THE ITALIAN
RENAISSANCE

HANGING
GARDEN

SMALL HERMITAGE

PAVILION HALL

LARGE ITALIAN
SKYLIGHT HALL

OLD HERMITAGE

KNIGHTS' HALL

HERMITAGE
THEATRE

NEW HERMITAGE

MAIN STAIRCASE

WINTER CANAL

FIRST WINTER
BRIDGE

RAPHAEL LOGGIAS

ЭРМИТАЖ
Альбом (на английском языке)

Издательство «Альфа Колор»
197101, С.-Петербург, Каменноостровский пр., д. 15
Тел./факс: +7(812) 336-25-27, 336-25-28
e-mail: yarkiy@sovintel.spb.ru

Вывод пленок ЗАО «Голанд», С.-Петербург
Отпечатано в типографии «Мультипринт Северо-Запад», С.-Петербург

1882 23 860020 66